Photographers Credits

Jorge Barquet, 15,17
Fernando Cordero, 49, 50, 51, 52, 53, 54, 55, 56,
89, 91, 92, 93, 94
Paul Czitrom B., 33, 35, 36, 38, 41, 43, 45, 47
Lucio Muniain, 63, 64, 65, 81
Mario Mutschlechner, 27, 29, 30, 46
Ignacio Urquiza, 39
Arturo Zavala, cover, 18, 19, 21, 22, 23, 25, 37, 60,
61, 67, 69, 70, 71, 72, 73, 75, 77, 78, 79

Editorial Director USA
Pierantonio Giacoppo

Chief Editor of Collection
Maurizio Vitta

Publishing Coordinator
Franca Rottola

Graphic Design
Paola Polastri

Editing
Jesse Oona Nickerson

Colour-separation
Litofilms Italia, Bergamo

Printing
Poligrafiche Bolis, Bergamo

First published November 1996

Copyright 1996
by l'Arca Edizioni

ISBN 88-7838-019-9

de Yturbe arquitectos

de Yturbe arquitectos
Dwelling versus Building

Preface by
Lucio Muniain

Introduction by
Enrique Martin-Moreno C.

Contents

Preface

by Lucio Muniain

The work of Jose de Yturbe has been renowned for almost thirty years. Early in his career, he was recognized principally for his houses and also for several public buildings. As his architecture matured, architectural competitions started to fill up his schedule, and the development of office buildings and administrative offices followed. Shortly thereafter came a period of hotels and golf clubs, although De Yturbe was always busy with smaller projects as well. Small in terms of size not of importance or relevance. In fact in the mid-eighties, he was developing the Torre Alta Office Building in Monterrey, as well as the Condumex Office Headquarters, and at the time of the Westin Regina Hotel, and the Malinalco Golf Club, he was also working on the Casa de Las Palapas.

In spite of the office's relatively short history, a monograph documenting its activity is now desirable. Up to now, anybody who wanted to know something about De Yturbe's buildings and projects had to turn to periodicals. This monograph, like many books of its kind, is divided in two parts: a detailed catalogue of selected works followed by a complete work list, and a description of each work that tries to familiarize the reader with De Yturbe Arquitectos' unknown vernacular minimalism. Unknown meaning not yet published.

But who is actually responsible for this book? Who is De Yturbe Arquitectos? Perhaps these questions must be answered since the history of this office by today's standards, is relatively unusual. The firm De Yturbe Arquitectos began with the separation of Jose De Yturbe from Sordo Madaleno Arquitectos in 1993. In that same year, I was lucky enough to be invited by De Yturbe to join him as partner principal of his firm, and of course, I knew exactly where I was going, since De Yturbe had already led a flourishing practice for almost thirty years. This, practically meant that all the building commissions were already there for me, allowing me to step beyond the tiresome beginning of the architectural career. On the other hand, it meant an entry into a large practice with all its risks, pressures and enormous responsibilities. I use the word practice because unlike many architects of today, who are interested in theoretical issues, we did not begin our work in an academic context—we began in the context of practice. We have progressed slowly from this beginning, to develop a theoretical basis for our work that takes in account the daily needs of practice, as well as a larger spectrum of possibilities. This issue is a binding answer to the building task and its conditions, not as an individual signature or gesture, but as a representative view of this office's work.

We see drawing in architecture as a tool, not as an end in and of itself. We draw to design, to test approaches, and to generate ideas.

Our presentation drawings are very similar to our sketches, only more carefully constructed. They are also a tool, to help our clients, and the public, to understand better our buildings' basic design intentions. They are, in fact, done very quickly, after careful composition. Their abstraction focuses on the fundamental compositional strategies that are a signature of de Yturbe arquitectos.

Architecture, for us, is an opportunity to reunite simple pleasures, such as light, air, view, colour, natural beauty, and simplicity. Over the years, filled by ideas, we have always followed the premise of "less is more". This idea has been so marked in our works, that we tended to open the doors of minimalism. In Mexico, we believe it is a highly common thought or factor. Many constructions all over the city are built in a very high degree of cheapness, and it is very common to hear people talking of a minimalism that exists only because of their beliefs in simplicity. It is very tragic to think of architecture as minimal for economic or sociological reasons, but most of the thinking concerning construction in Mexico, as well as in many places all over the world, is focused on lack of ornament since ornament is often confused with craftwork.

We often receive comments that our architecture is not minimal because of its high degree of intimacy, but we are certain that not all minimalism must be frozen cold. We believe that architecture, as the realm of creating spaces in which people live part or all their lives, must have that feeling, of "home" a feeling that will develop and stay in their minds as a premise of truth.

When we approach a new site, we focus on the topography as natural architecture that will guide the architectural path by itself. We create an architecture that is subordinated by its surroundings, that does not impose on the natural landscape.

We do not believe in affirmations of principles, or manifestations that announce cultural revolutions, in declarations of loyalty to one or other of those tendencies or movements that expect as an answer to represent or homogenize architecture.

We also do not believe in the arbitrariness of giving generalizing advice, or even worst, of assembling a catalogue of technical rules and regulations, or even in the fact that anyone can be or feel authorized to do architecture and judge when it is good or bad.

When we talk about architecture we believe there is only one method: to transmit a simple message, to have a clear understanding of the work either plastically or functionally.

Our only way to comunicate is through the work itself.

Building and meaning are one.

Dwelling versus Building

by Enrique Martin-Moreno C.

Through the pages of the *Burried Mirror*, Carlos Fuentes gave us a conciliatory vision of the history of the Latin American nations that helps us understand Mexican culture. He explained that the, wisely named, New World was once uninhabited. It was probably through the Bering Straight that the first inhabitants entered the continent, 40,000 or 50,000 years ago. Some travelled south and settled in the Mesoamerican region, (what we now call Mexico), and developed such cultures as the Olmec, Mayan, Zapotecan, Toltec, and finally the Aztec. These civilizations reigned in this land for more than twenty centuries. Then in the XVI Century, the Spanish *conquistadores* came to settle in this land, bringing with them the inherited cultures of the first Iberians, Fenicians, Celts, Greeks, Carthaginians, Romans, but most important of all, they brought with them the strong Moorish influence of the Islamic culture and Christianity. It is this mixture of cultures, explains Fuentes, that constitutes Mexican culture, and it is strongly reflected in Mexican vernacular architecture.

It was Luis Barragán, a self-instructed architect, who first understood this essential quality of Mexican culture and, by abstracting the essence of vernacular space in his works of the early 1940s, he created a Minimalist Style, that constituted a strong critical front against the International Style that dominated the Mexican architectural field from the 1930s on. Barragán's architecture joined by Matías Goeritz's paintings and sculptures established the Minimalist Movement, considered one of the most important artistic episodes of the XX Century in Mexico since Muralism.

Many architects, disenchanted by the sterility of the International Style, joined the movement throughout the 1960s. 1968, a year of social and political turmoil in Mexico, was a very important year for the movement, for it not only saw the creation of Barragán's world-famous San Cistobal House and Stables, and the consolidation of the movement with Ricardo Legorreta's Camino Real Hotel in Mexico City, the first large-scale building within the movement, but also, it was the first time that freedom of composition based on Barragán's minimal planes faced the structural grid, a matter that to this day remains unsolved; but 1968 also witnessed the beginning of José de Yturbe's professional career.

Since his first commissions, de Yturbe showed his affinity with Barragán's works, from them, he learned the importance of intimacy, privacy and serenity of interior spaces. De Yturbe found that courtyards could serve this purpose, with the acoustic presence of water, reflecting the influence of Islamic architecture found throughout the southern regions of the Iberean Peninsula, and there fore has developed a rich repertory of courtyards throughout his works. He also learned the use of colours, suggested to Barragán by Matías Goeritz and by the influential painter Jesús Reyes Ferreira (who came to be known as Chucho Reyes). De Yturbe inherited Barragán's architectural language, a reinterpretation of Mexican vernacular architecture which is reflected in the materials: clay, cobbles and *recinto* (a black volcanic rock) of the floors; rough textures on the walls, like the ones found in the colonial rural houses and convents; the timber beams that support the roofs. To this simple pallet of materials, which profits from the craftsmanship of the Mexican worker, de Yturbe incorporated the use of tiled sloping roofs and *palapas*, found abundantly in Mexican vernacular architecture. But, most importantly, de Yturbe proved that he understood the spirit of discovery of what Barragán liked to refer to as an "architectural striptease", in other words the interior is unveiled as the visitor progresses from room to room.

An important aspect to fully understand de Yturbe's works is that the interior perceptive process precedes the exterior object.

Like Mies, de Yturbe concieves a space through planes; but in the design process, a line generates the space instead of a point, i.e. the wall contains the space and is given individual plastic value whereas the structure is concealed within the plasticity of the walls.

The emotional incitement of the spaces in de Yturbe's works is more sensorial than optic, this is achieved by the textures, the craftwork and colour of the materials, together with the sound of splashing water and the tamed use of natural light and vegetation. All these architectural elements provide warmth to space without using ornament, and reflect de Yturbe's focus on long-term living in his works. The use of natural lighting gives the sun a key role in the appreciation of space, i.e. it changes the emotions evoked by the quality of the space throughout the whole day.

When de Yturbe approaches a site, he does not see an empty lot: the design process is subordinated to the existing vegetation and the surrounding constructions, thus the works appear to belong to their context. The vegetation is allowed to grow freely, and by doing so, it becomes united with the architectural work itself, as they age hand in hand. The surrounding landscape is integrated to the interior of the work, for it has a visual dominance through carefully placed openings in the walls. De Yturbe's works represent a truce between man and nature.

All this explains the principle behind de Yturbe's work: *dwelling versus building.* As a disciple of Barragán's spirit, de Yturbe follows his words upon recieving the Pritzker Prize in 1980: "*In alarming proportions the following words have disappeared from architectural publications: beauty, inspiration, magic, sorcery, enchantment, and also serenity, mystery, silence, privacy, astonishment. All of these words have found a loving home in my soul.*" De Yturbe recently invited one of Mexico's most talented young architects: Lucio Muniain, who has worked for him since the age of 18, and is established in the firm of de Yturbe Arquitectos since 1994. Together, de Yturbe and Muniain have created spaces with intangible qualities such as Barragán referred to. So I leave you now to your brief visit through their works, and I am sure that you will find it very hard to imagine that these were once blank pieces of paper pasted on de Yturbe Arquitectos' drawing boards.

WITHDRAWN

Works

House in San Angel

Ground area
800.00 sq/m

Constructed area
690.00 sq/m

Beginning construction date
1975

Opening date
1975

Architectural Design
de Yturbe Arquitectos

Structural Project
José Luís Camba

Architectural supervision
José de Yturbe

Project Development
1974

Interior Design
Dupuis

Text
Enrique Martin-Moreno

San Angel, a residential suburb, is located in the south side of the city. Once a rural setting, San Angel got its name from the large *hacienda* that dominated the area. Although the stone paved streets are quiet and peaceful, the houses of San Angel live within walls that protect the private interior spaces. This house, built while Barragán was still active, is almost monastic in its private spaces behind its protective walls. The house presents a massive wall to the calm and unperturbed street of San Angel, while a wooden door admits the visitor to a passage-way, between two high converging walls, that lead through a narrow vertical opening to the terra-cotta paved atrium of the house.

This atrium presents large openings in two of its walls allowing space to flow and unite with the luxuriant vegetation of the wonderfully landscaped backyard. In one of the corners of the courtyard, the terra-cotta floor slopes imperceptibly to form a shallow pool that reflects not only the massive walls but the exuberant foliage of the backyard that has grown freely throughout the years invading the plain walls of the courtyard and integrating itself to the magical ambiance of this minimalist space.

One passes by this courtyard sheltered by the volumes of the house that are projected over one's head, giving the impression that two of the walls of the courtyard are suspended in mid-air.

One enters the house through a vestibule that is ornamented only by a sculptoric staircase that ascends to the more private reaches of the house located on the second level. From the vestibule, one can enter either into the dining room with its picture window that opens completely, uniting the interior space to the courtyard, or into the living room by descending a flight of steps that end in a converging slot that provides a selected view of the courtyard. The living room has a balustrade opposite to the large sliding window that looks upon the rich foliage of the backyard.

WITHDRAWN

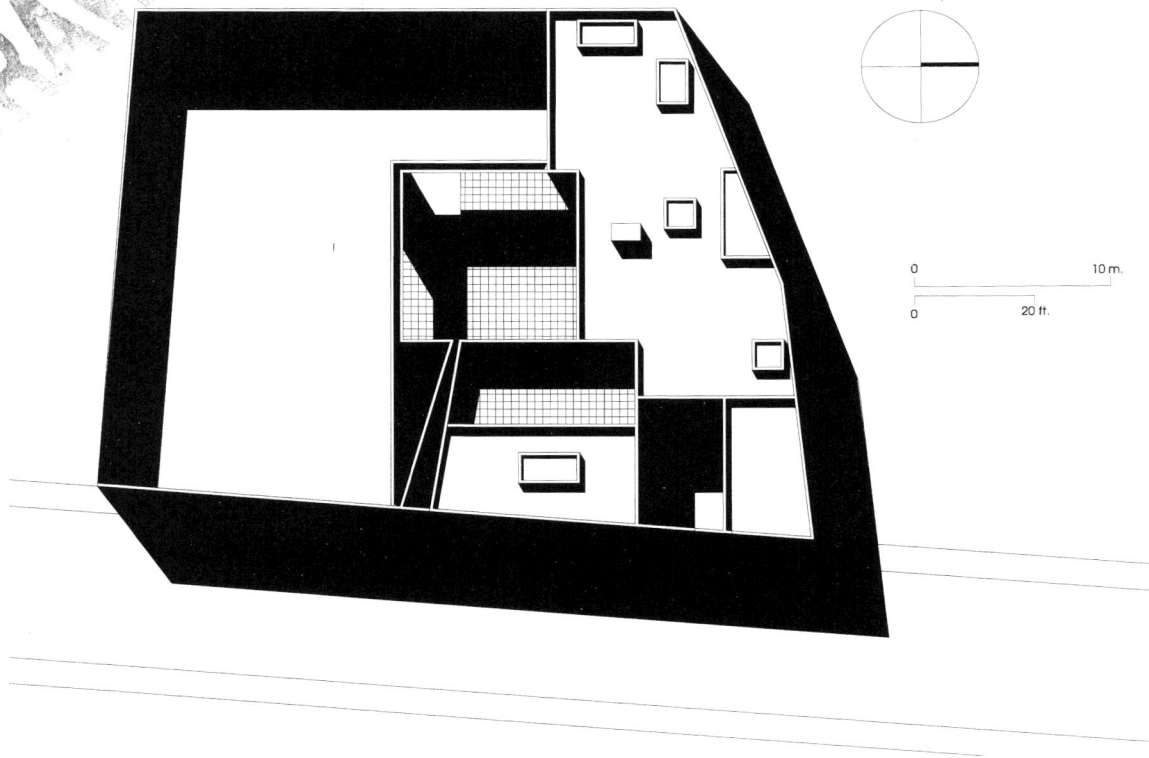

Site plan and plan
of the building.
Opposite page, detail
of the building.

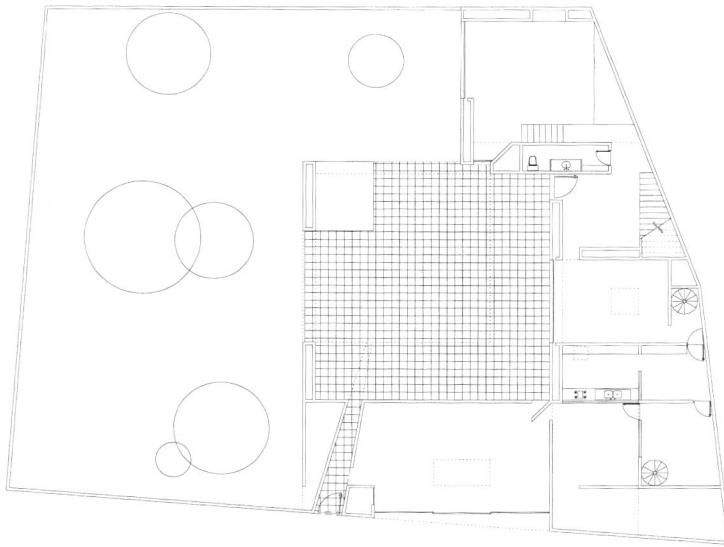

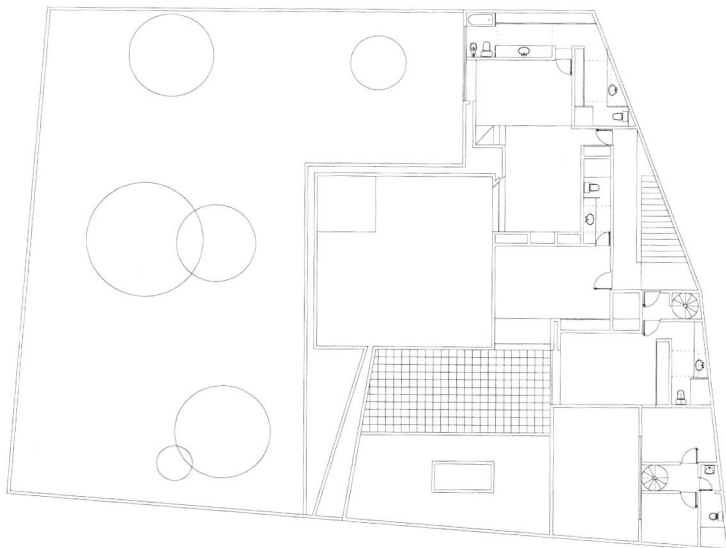

0   10 m.

0   20 ft.

Opposite page, partial
view of the entrance
path.

View of the living room
and, bottom of page,
view of the garden.

House in Bosques de Las Lomas

Ground area
1,490.00

Contructued area
680.000 sq/m

Beginning construction date
1974

Opening date
1975

Architectural Design
de Yturbe Arquitectos

Structural Project
Jaime Loyola

Architectural supervision
José de Yturbe

Text
Enrique Martin-Moreno

Bosques de las Lomas which means "Hill Forests" is a very exclusive neighbourhood in the west of Mexico City. The houses are surrounded by protective walls and fences, thus forcing the architecture to become drawn inward. This house, contemporary to Barragán's Casa Gilardi, accepts the quality of its surroundings and lives within itself creating two private views in the interior of the house: the courtyard at the entrance, and the beautifully landscaped backyard.

Continuing with what Barragán liked to refer to as an "architectural striptease" one enters this suburban house to find a narrow flight of steps between two high, protectively massed walls which lead down and around a corner to a terra-cotta paved courtyard. It is upon reaching the landing to this narrow staircase that a glimpse of the great atrium is revealed through a carefully placed square opening in the wall. Suddenly, when you reach the bottom of the steps, you are left without the protection of the walls, and, as Ferdinand Bac once wrote, "with the force of a revelation" you fully discover this very abstract and minimalist courtyard.

As if trying to fill the space left by the square opening in the wall, a stone cube seems to emerge from the ground in one of the corners of the courtyard flooding the courtyard with water and turning it into a very large and surreal fountain.

One of de Yturbe's main prerogatives is to let the vegetation grow freely. In this case the foliage has grown and aged with the courtyard thus creating a sensation that it will become more enchanting as time goes by.

Although serene and simple, the textures of the plain massive walls and the damp floor, with the added splendour provided by the water and vegetation, bewitch the visitors of this house. Through this everchanging game of light and colour, de Yturbe lets nature take its course knowing that it will never repeat itself. Different every second of the day, this courtyard is rediscovered every time it is visited. Filling the spectator with surprise, this atrium becomes a poetic celebration of life.

One passes by this courtyard sheltered by one of the volumes of the house that is corbelled above one's head and enters a low and protective vestibule where a staircase begins its descent to the more private areas of the house. From the vestibule one can enter a living room with a large window that provides a complete view of the atrium. By going down a flight of steps one reaches another living room with a generous view of the wonderfully landscaped backyard.

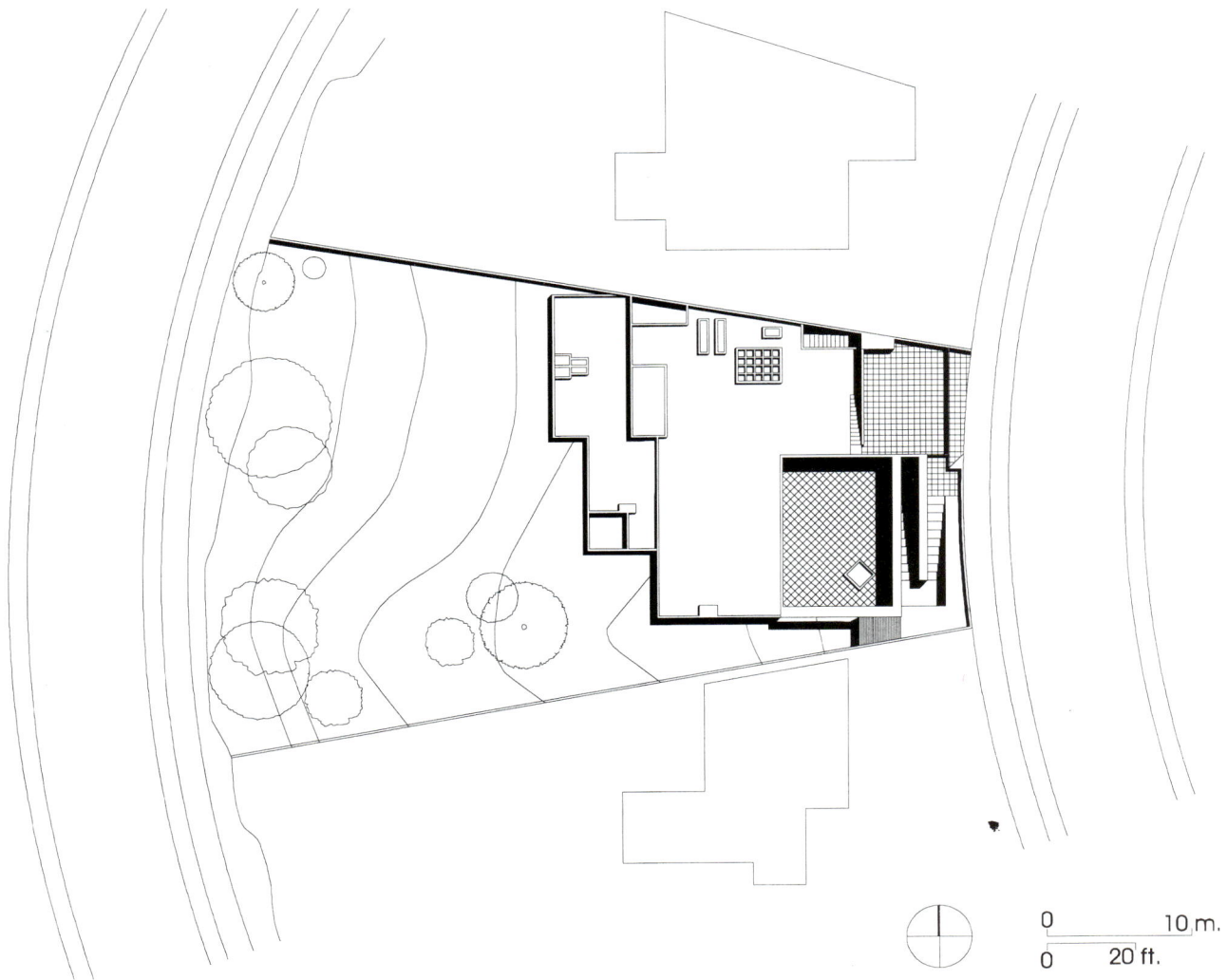

View of the patio.
Opposite page, view
of the outside showing
a detail of the wooden
roof and, bottom
of page, the site plan.

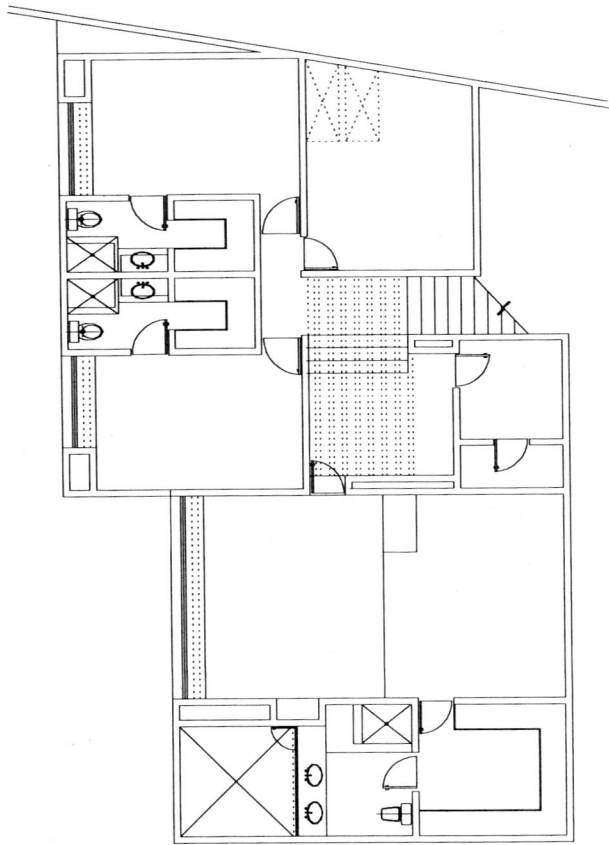

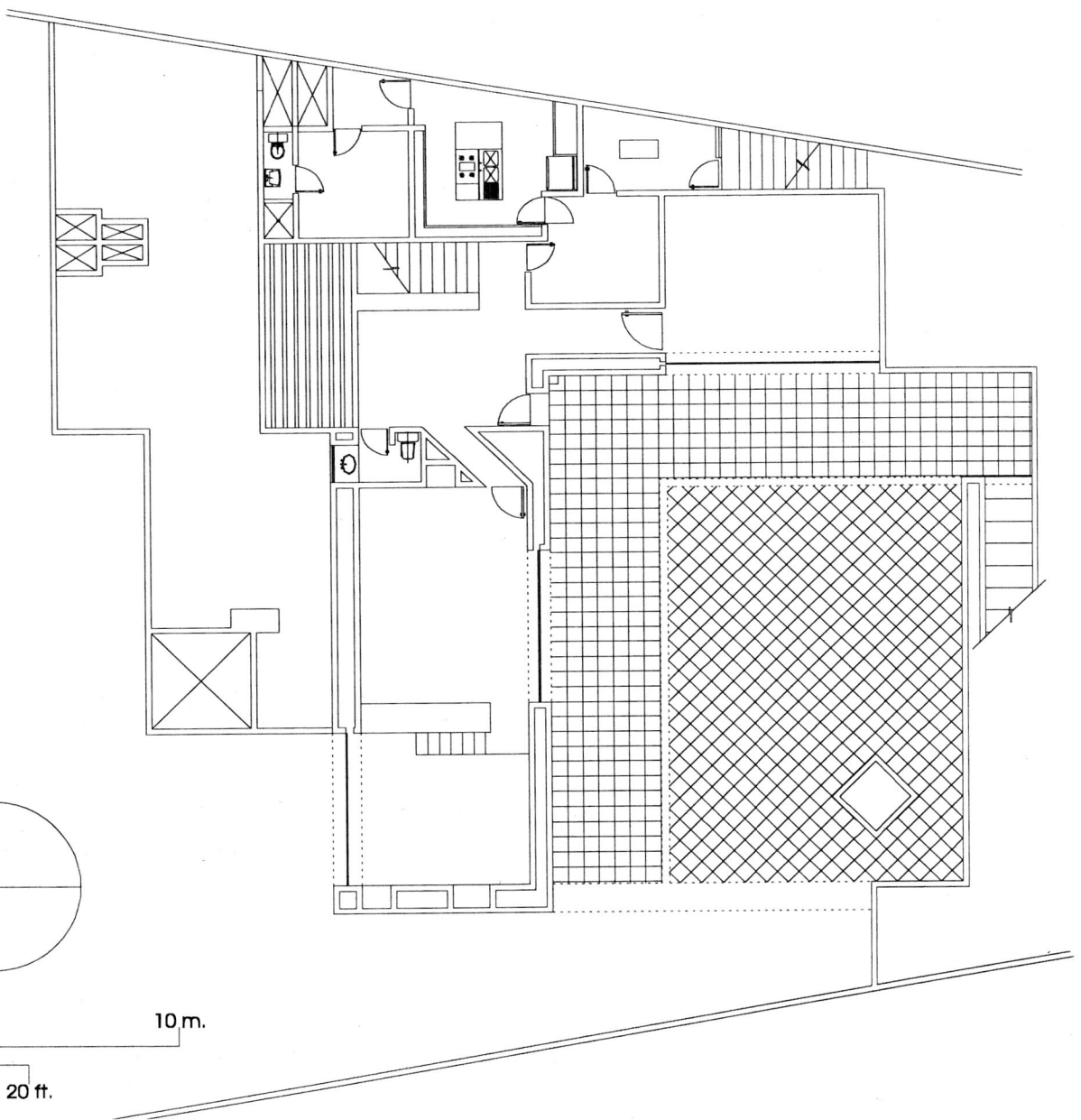

0   10 m.

0   20 ft.

Interior view of the house and, below, the staircase that descends from the entrance. Opposite page, plans of both floors of the building.

Condumex Office Headquarters

Owner
Grupo Condumex

Ground area
12,315.00 sq/m

Constructed area
2,405.00 sq/m

Beginning construction date
1979

Opening date
1981

Architectural Design
de Yturbe Arquitectos

Structural Project
Jaime Loyola

Electrical Project
Arellano Ingenieros

Architectural supervision
José de Yturbe

Project Development
1979

Interior Design
José de Yturbe

Text
Enrique Martin-Moreno

The Condumex Corporative Headquarters are situated in a lot of what used to be Carmen Convent during colonial times, located in the south of Mexico City, in an area known as Chimalistac, from the church located in that area. It is a field occupied only by trees and an old colonial townhouse, which de Yturbe remodeled for the use of Condumex as the Centre for the Study of Mexican History. One enters this complex from the stone-paved street of Chimalistac to a long drive way that lets you see the beauty of tree-covered fields before taking you to the underground parking lot. Here you find a staircase that ascends to a courtyard. De Yturbe first designed this courtyard with slanted walls forming oblique slots through which one would enter, but during construction, realizing the aggressiveness of the triangular walls and acute angles, he dramatically changed the courtyard and gave his client one of the world's most intriguing and serene minimalist spaces: an empty cube within a cube of massive vivid red walls.

An "L" shaped wall, painted with a colour known as 'Mexican pink', momentarily prevents the visitor from discovering the atrium, ornamented only by a cluster of of dried palm tree trunks.

A square opening in one of the walls of the atrium with a large massive wooden door admits the visitor to a vestibule with a large reception area, stairs that ascend to the second floor, and office space to both sides. On the second floor, a circulation walkway that leads to the large, naturally illuminated waiting area on the first floor, takes you to another large office area on the east side of the building. On the west side, one finds an ample office that looks down on an outside terra-cotta paved patio with a long narrow fountain that resembles the horse troughs of the rural *haciendas*.

Taking a look at the floor plan, one discovers the bizarre design of the building which is born from de Yturbe's desire to keep the existing trees in order to integrate them into the whole design. A task he later mastered and repeated in the Westin Regina Hotel in Puerto Vallarta (1990-1991).

View of the entrance
from patio.

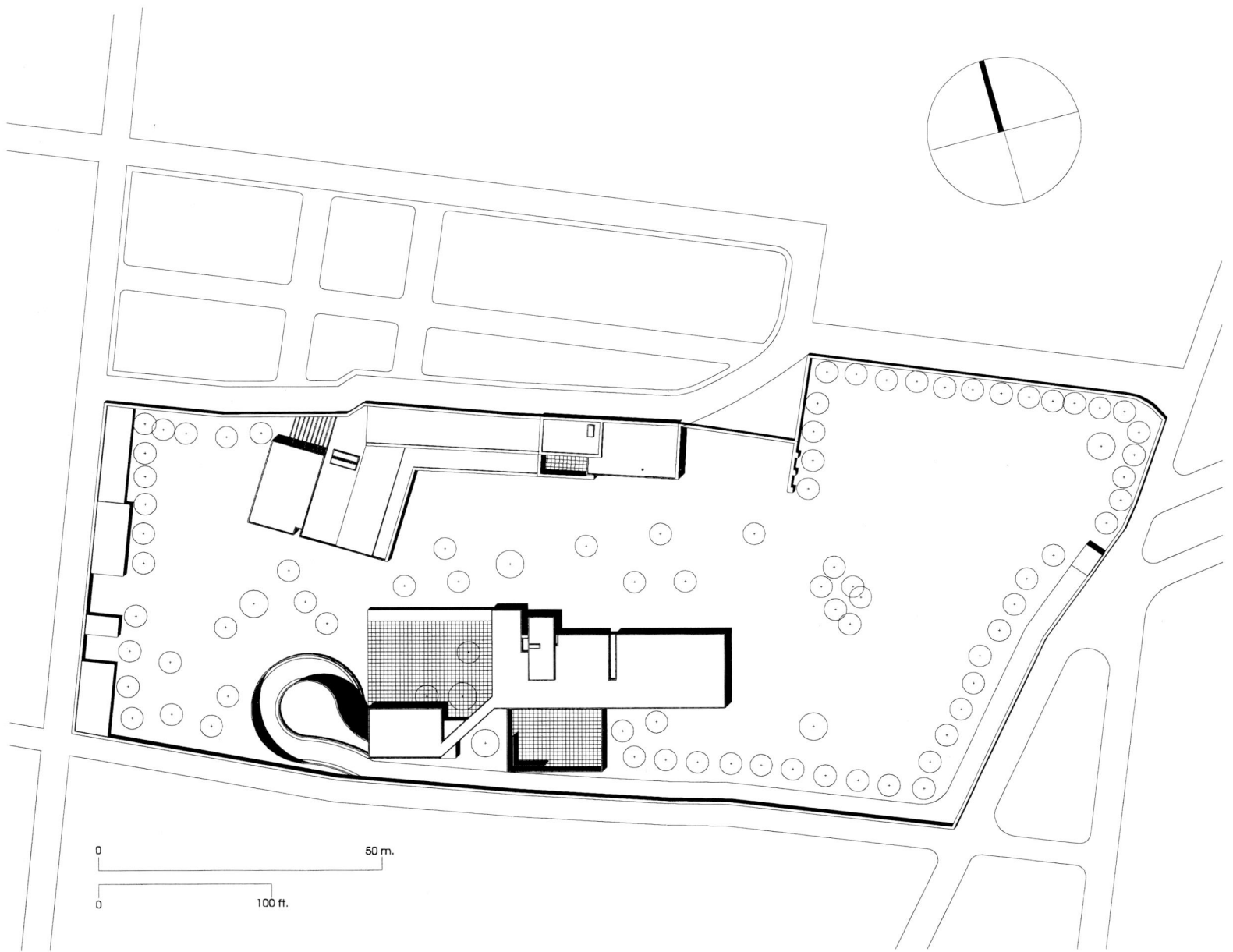

0 _____ 50 m.

0 _____ 100 ft.

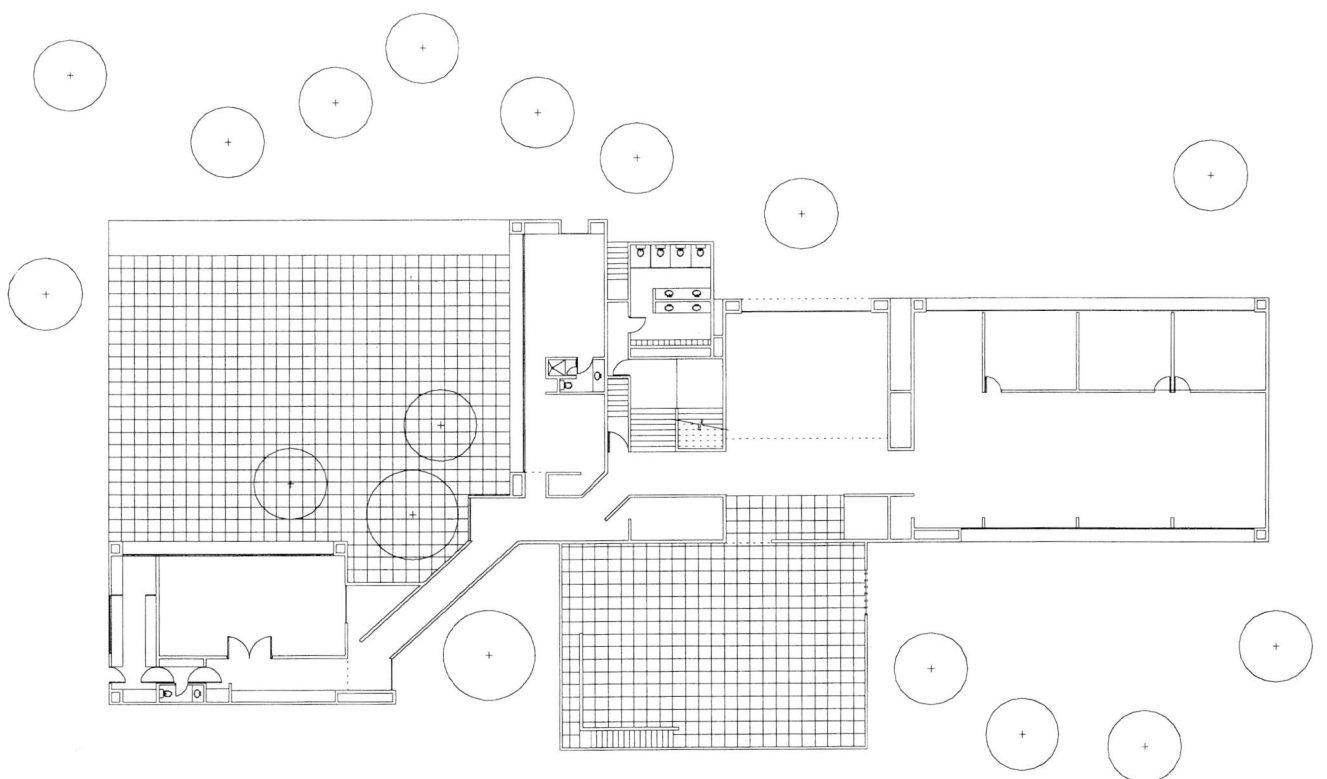

Entrance passage and
one of the building
facades and, opposite
page, site plan and plan
of the building.

View of the north
facade.

Casa de Las Palapas

Ground area
20,000.00 sq/m

Constructed area
960.000 sq/m

Project Development
1987

Beginning construction date
1988

Opening date
1989

Architectural Design
de Yturbe Arquitectos

Structural Project
José de Yturbe

Electrical Project
José de Yturbe

Hydrological Project
José de Yturbe

Construction
José de Yturbe

Architectural supervision
José de Yturbe

Text
Enrique Martin-Moreno

A *palapa* is a conical roof covered by dried royal palm tree leaves cut and assembled during the new moon, due to the lunar cycle followed by the royal palm tree in its growth pattern. It is a descendant of the *bohío*, the primitive huts of the Yucatán natives and it provides many acoustic and thermal advantages.

This house is immersed in the tropical jungle of the Mexican Pacific Coast, in the State of Nayarit, an hour's drive north of Puerto Vallarta. It is, in all respects, utterly integrated with the site.

The house, made of seven cylindrical cells roofed by *palapas,* was designed spontaneously. A single cell design was made: an empty cube inside a massive cylinder roofed by a *palapa*. It was directly on the site, that de Yturbe decided the location and orientation of each cell. The cylindrical shape of the cells allows groupings in any desired way.

One enters the house to a courtyard circumscribed by seventeen massive cylindrical pillars painted with faded Mexican pink. The courtyard leads to the main *palapa* which houses the dining room and the living room, that face the setting sun. Most of the furniture is built-in and the rest is simple and in harmony with the architecture. Giant seashells adorn the minimalist interior of the main *palapa*. The pathways to the other *palapas* are immersed in the natural foliage of the site. They unite you with the elements, in an attempt to isolate you from the rest of civilization. The bedrooms, lacking crystal windows, have beatiful vistas of the Pacific Ocean through carefully placed openings in the massive cylindrical walls.

External view of
the three main
constructions showing
a detail of the entrance
ramp.

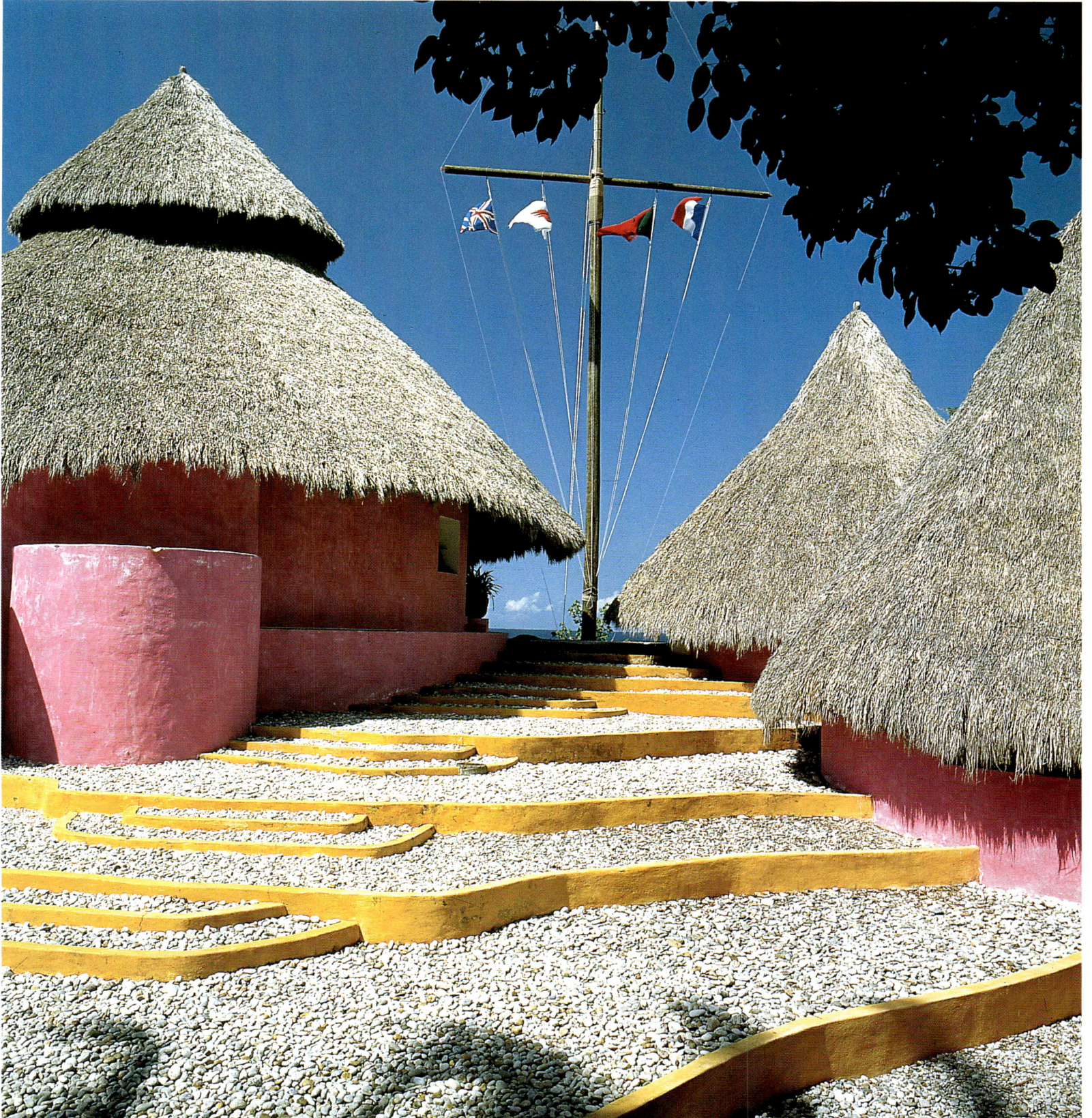

Top of page, living and
dining room floor plans;
bottom of page, site
plan of the entire
complex.

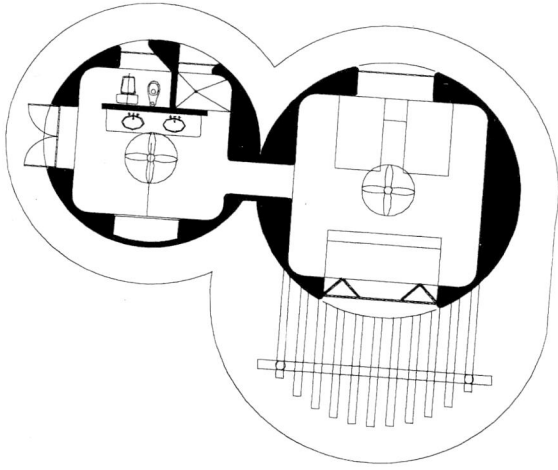

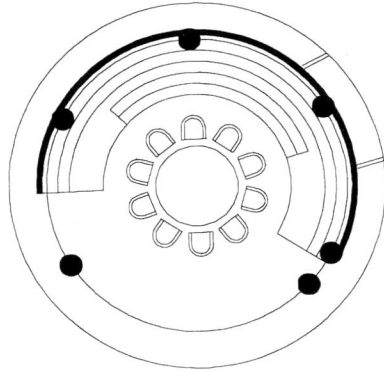

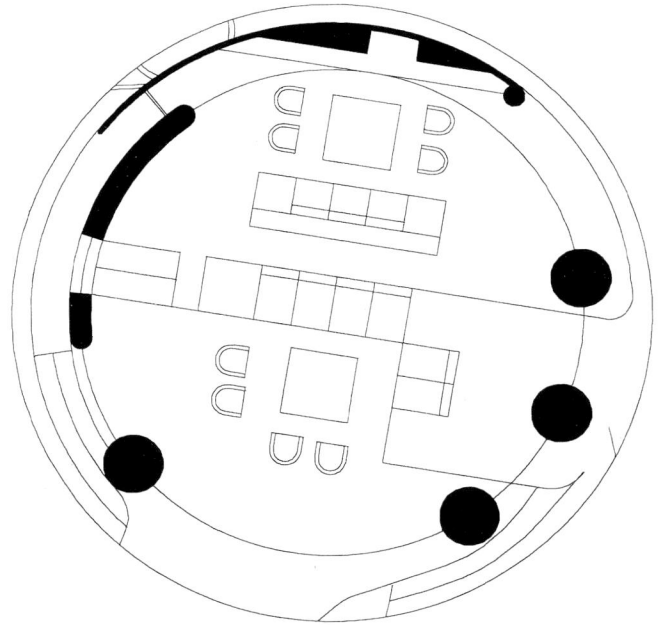

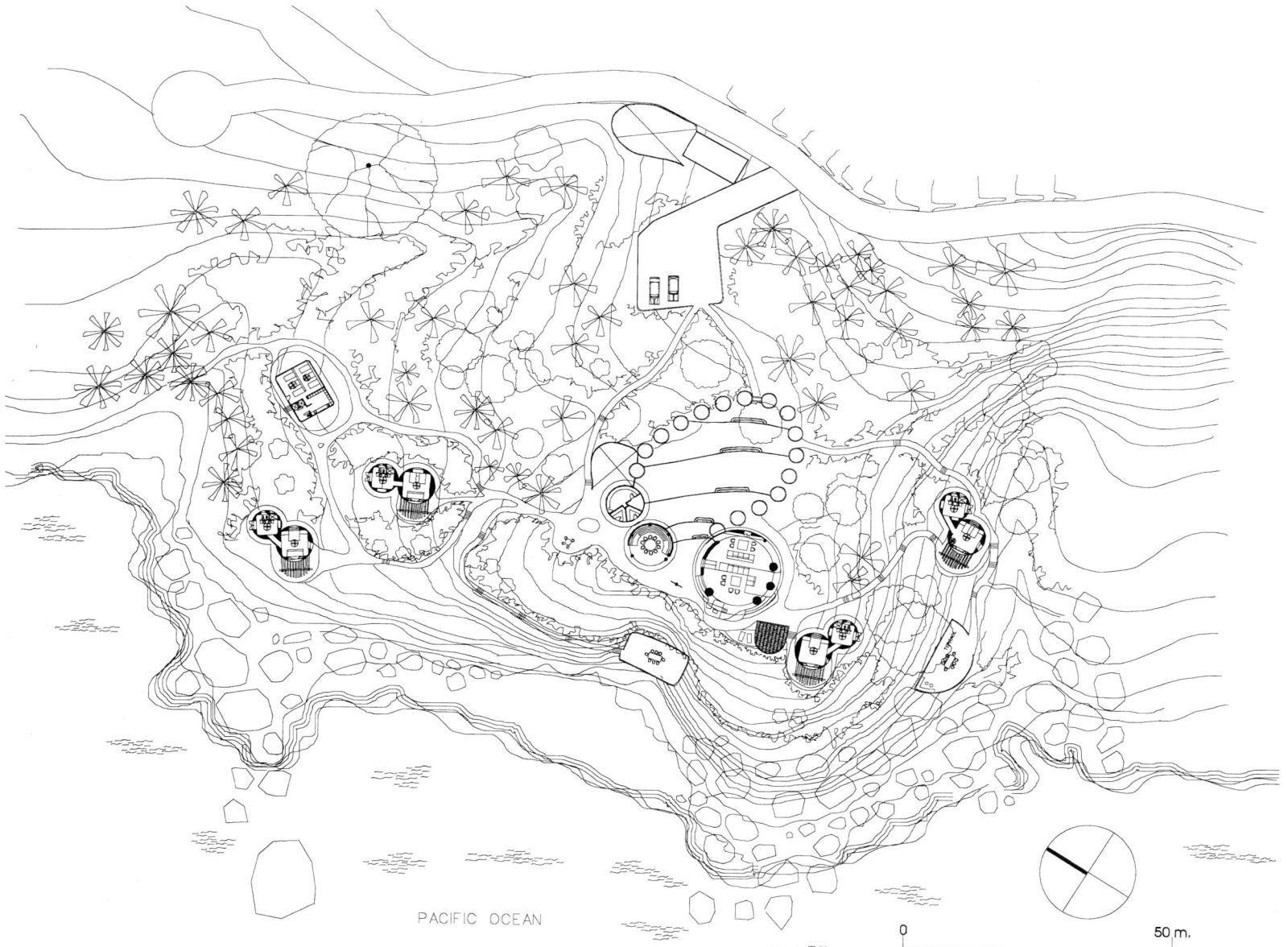

PACIFIC OCEAN

0

50 m.

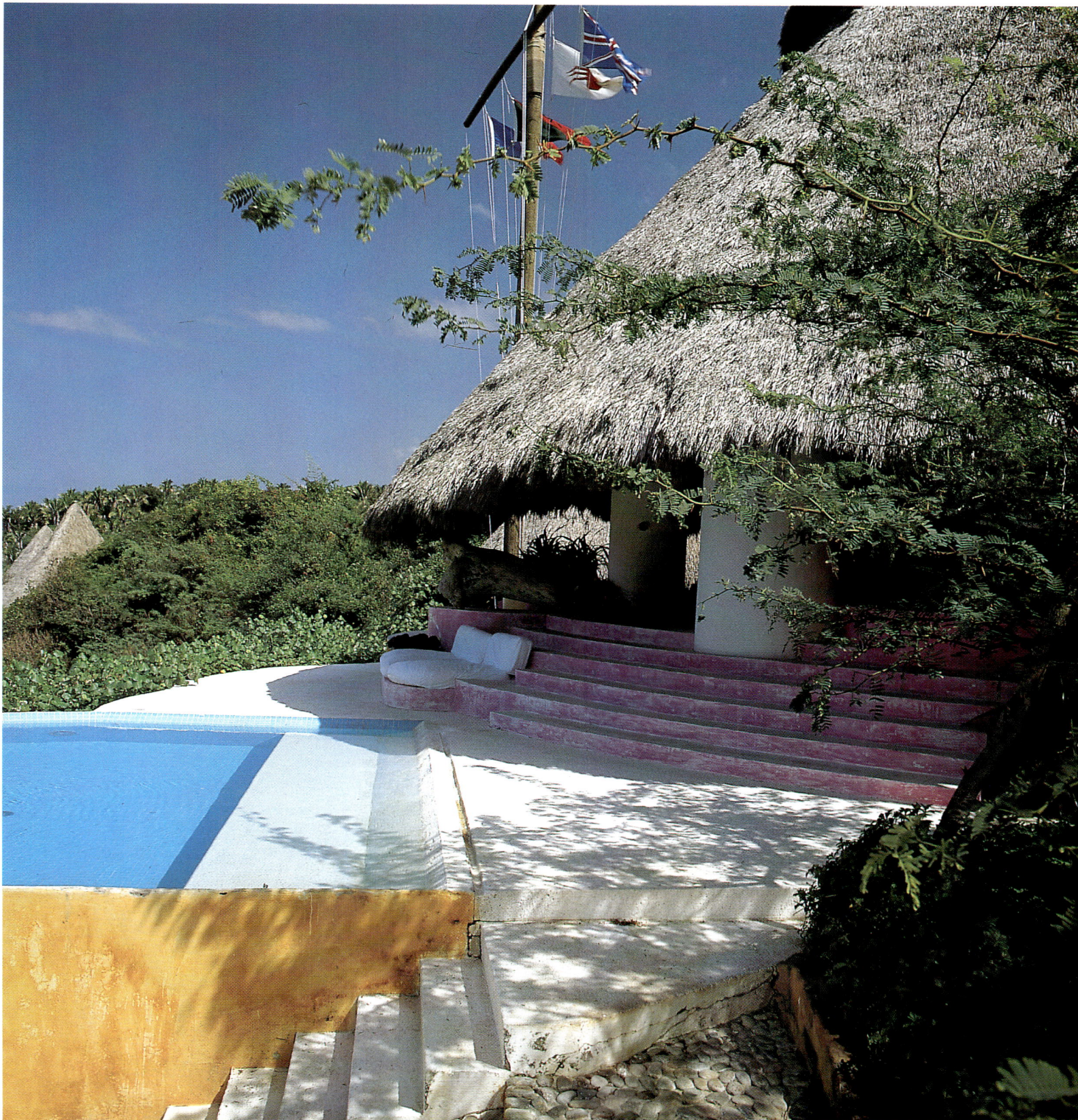

View of the swimming pool behind the main building.

Two details of
the roof's elaborate
architecture.

Two internal views
underlining the peculiar
interaction between
architecture
and environment.

The Westin Regina Resort Hotel

Owner
Bancomer, S.A.

Operator
Westin Hotels

Ground area
85,500.00 sq/m

Constructed area
80,000.00 sq/m

Beginning construction date
1989

Opening date
1993

Architectural Design
Javier Sordo Madaleno, José de Yturbe
Jorge Isaías, Hector Meza, Jorge Flores
Sordo Madaleno Arquitectos

Structural Project
José Luís Camba

Electrical Project
Arellano Ingeniería

Hydrological Project
G.H.A. Gutiérrez Tello y Asociados

Construction
GUTSA, CIEMSA

Architectural supervision
Sordo Madaleno Arquitectos

Project Development
1988

Interior Design
IntraDesign, Los Angeles, C.A.

Landscape Architecture
Eduard Stone Jr. & Associates (EDSA)

Air Conditioning
Calefacción y Ventilación, S.A. (CYVSA)

Competition date
1988

Construction Coordinator
RUAL, S.A.

Text
Enrique Martin-Moreno

The town of Puerto Vallarta is located in the Bahía de Banderas, meaning the "bay of flags", on the Mexican Pacific Coast. Unlike many tourist resorts, Puerto Vallarta is a colonial town that has a strong vernacular architectural tradition. Puerto Vallarta has a tropical climate, warm all year round but with a heavy rainy season, thus the sloping tiled roofs found throughout the whole town. The site for the hotel was a lot with a very dense palm grove.

The hotel, recalled by the Mexican press as the "encounter of man and nature", is located in the touristic area of the town, and was designed with the intention of isolating the guests from the bustle of the town, in the private and serene interior spaces of the compound. Also, the uncertainty as to the adjacent lots, at the time of the buildings' construction, made the hotel "turn its back" to the outside, to live from within and project itself toward the majestic Banderas Bay and the waters of the Pacific Ocean.

Although a study for a low, horizontal hotel was made, the desire to keep the existing palm trees made it impossible, so a vertical scheme was presented. When analysing a section of any of the buildings one finds that it is organized in modules three stories high. These modules were horizontally offset allowing the facade that faces the palm grove to have a slight inclination, that projects the interior space towards the sky. It also creates three-storey high tropically landscaped areas beside the walkways that look toward the outside of the compound, and allows these walkways to be in close contact with nature. These vegetated areas permit the walkways to the rooms to be naturally ventilated by protecting them from the strong rains of Puerto Vallarta. The motor lobby of the hotel is covered by a highly crafted sloping tiled roof.

From the motor lobby one enters the hotel through openings in three parallel Mexican pink walls. The lobby of the hotel is flooded by light through an extraordinary skylight hidden by three immense concrete beams perpendicular to roughly carved timber beams. The poured white concrete floor contrasts with the pebblestone handicrafted design of a sun in the centre of the lobby.

From the lobby by descending a wide flight of steps one gets a great view of the interior space: the pool area.

The organic design of the pool area was determined by the location of the palm trees, for only five percent of the existing palm trees were replanted within the compound, the rest were kept as they were found, integrating them completely to the design of the whole. This hotel exemplifies de Yturbe's great respect of nature and profound understanding of the site.

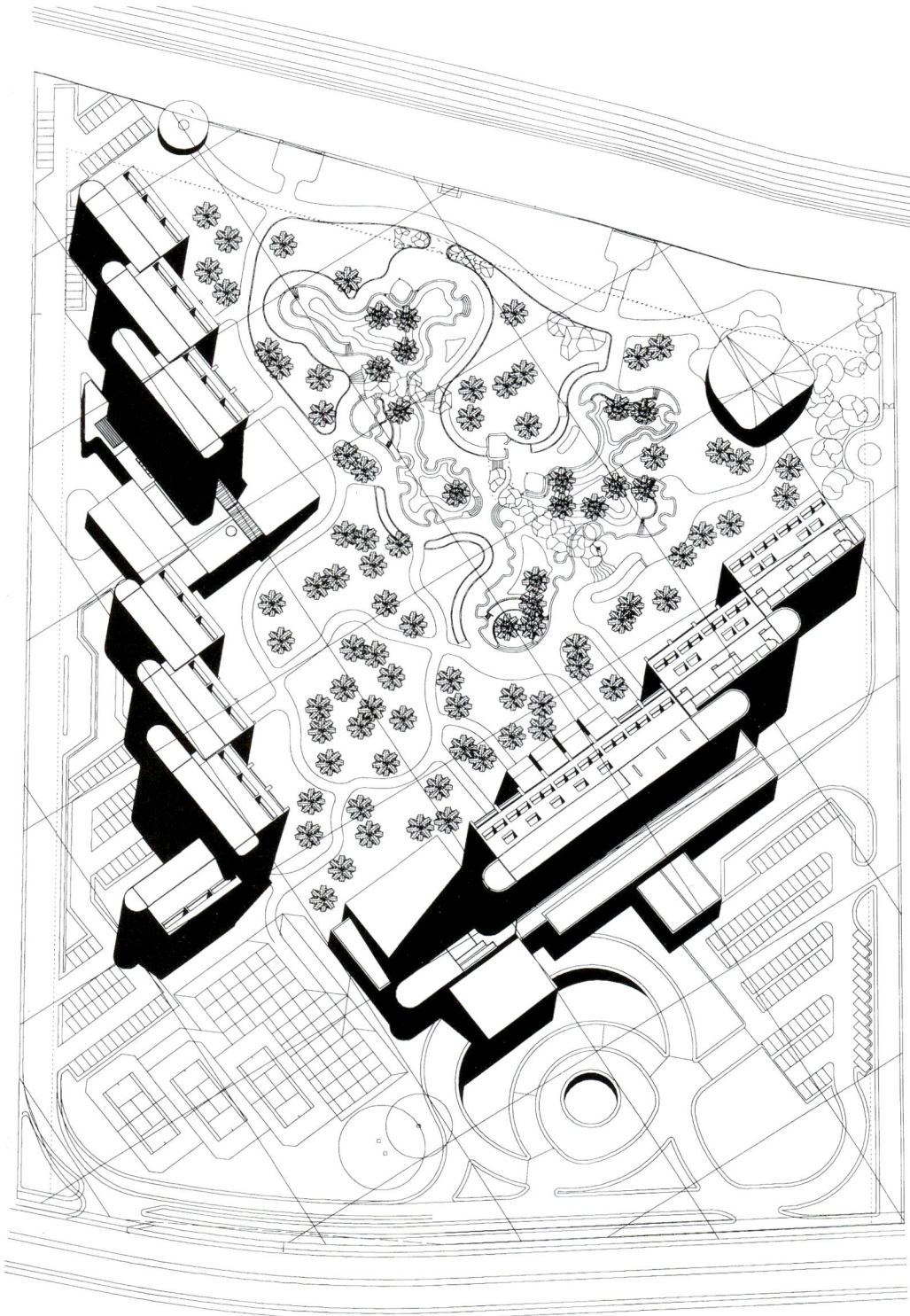

Site plan of the entire
complex and, opposite,
view of the buildings.

Section of the suites
and hotel lobby section
and opposite page,
an external view of
complex.

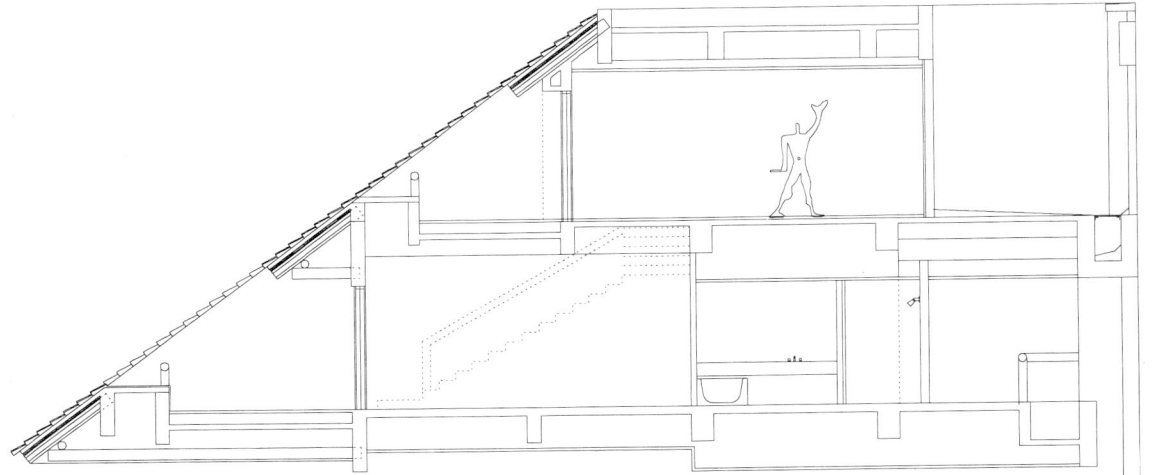

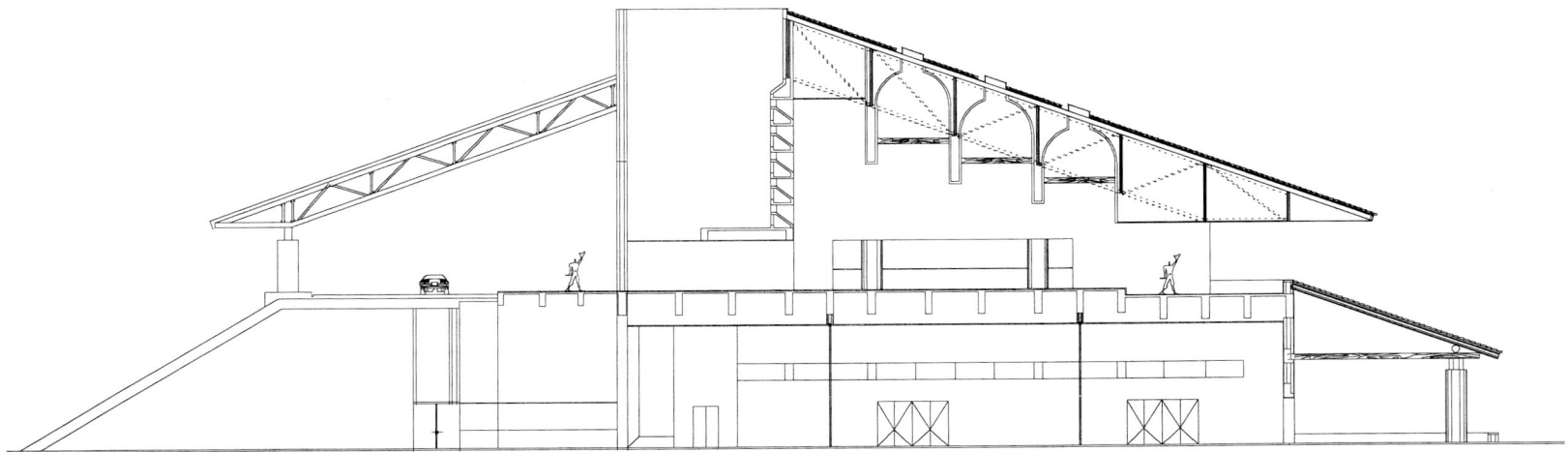

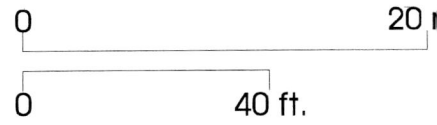

0

0   20 ft.

0   20 m

0   40 ft.

This page and opposite page, two interior views of the building.

Los Cabos, Baja California Sur,
Mexico, 1993

The Westin Regina Resort Hotel

Owner
Bancomer, S.A.

Operator
Westin Hotels

Ground area
120,000.00 sq/m

Constructed area
70,000.00 sq/m

Beginning construction date
1990

Opening date
1993

Architectural Design
Javier Sordo Madaleno,
José de Yturbe, B,
Humberto Mendoza,
Armando Zarraga,
José Vigil,
Armando Chávez.

Structural Project
Alejandro Fierro

Electrical Project
Arellano Ingeniería

Hydrological Project
Gutiérrez Tello y Asociados

Construction
Ingenieros Civiles Asociados (ICA)

Architectural supervision
Sordo Madaleno Arquitectos

Project Development
1989

Interior Design
División Diseño de Interiores (DDI)

Landscape Architecture
Sordo Madaleno Arquitectos

Air Conditioning
Calefacción y Ventilación, S.A. (CYVSA)

Competition date
1989

Construction Coordinator
RUAL, S.A.

Text
Enrique Martin-Moreno

The Baja California Peninsula is home to one of nature's most magical moments, the surrendering of the red sands of the Baja California Desert to the blue waters of the Sea of Cortés. It is here that we find a place known as the Cerro Colorado, the "Red Hill".

A depression in the centre of the Cerro Colorado creates a natural forum from where one can witness this astonishing spectacle.

It is in this natural forum that the Westin Regina Hotel emerges from the ground, a great wall, the most Mexican of architectural elements, as if trying to be the curtain of a surreal theatre.

This great curtain, painted to match the colours of the ochre sands, defies nature as it offsets the strong sea winds, stopping the erosion of the ground, allowing the formation of a microclimate of exuberant tropical foliage, an oasis in the middle of the desert.

Suddenly, the curtain opens. A rectangular opening in this remarkable wall that measures 6 stories high and 45 meters wide, frames an extraordinary view of the sea. The great wall acts as a boundary between the two environments: the natural desert and the oasis, and it is the pool area to invade this boundary in an attempt to unite with the waters of the sea.

The curve-line in the great wall allows the 236 hotel rooms to have an unsurmountable view of the Sea of Cortés while shortening the walkway that looks toward the mild climate of the oasis.

The monumental wall is again interrupted by a vertical slot that joins the oasis with the other main area of the complex: the condominiums. This area was designed with the intent to be perceived at a distance as a texture formed by the individual volumes of each of the condominiums.

The curved walkways that reach the condominiums breaks the tension of the right angled edges of the condominiums meanwhile reaching the desert in the transition.

Another remarkable space found in this complex is the restaurant located outside the great wall with an extraordinary view of the sea the hotel and the condominiums. This semi-cylindrical volume is entered through an overwhelming atrium with a gigantic, vividly coloured concrete lattice that hides the view in an attempt to surprise the visitor when entering the restaurant.

Site plan of the entire complex and below, detail of one the cylindrical towers overlooking the ocean.

Opposite, main facade of the building, from the "oasis".

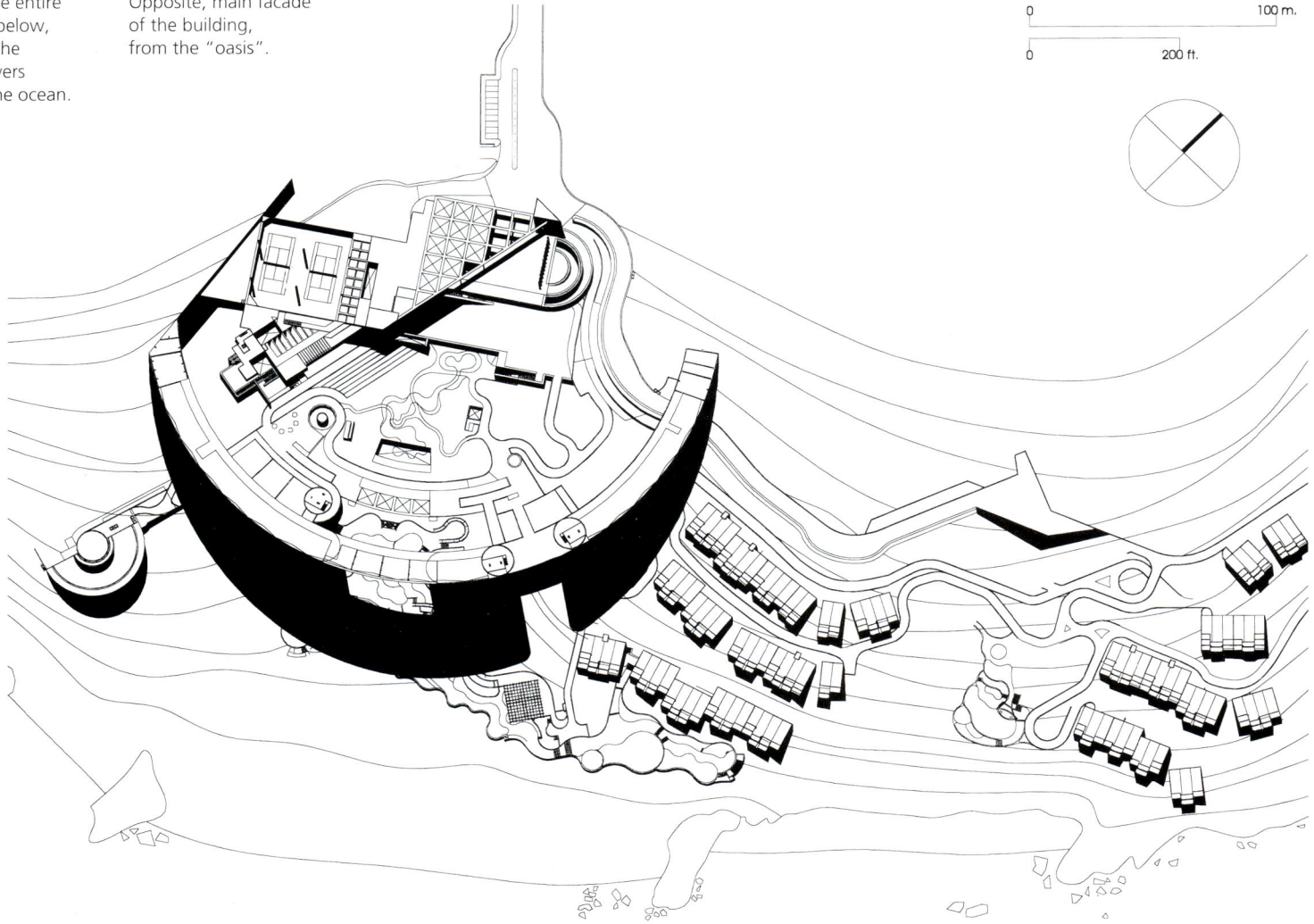

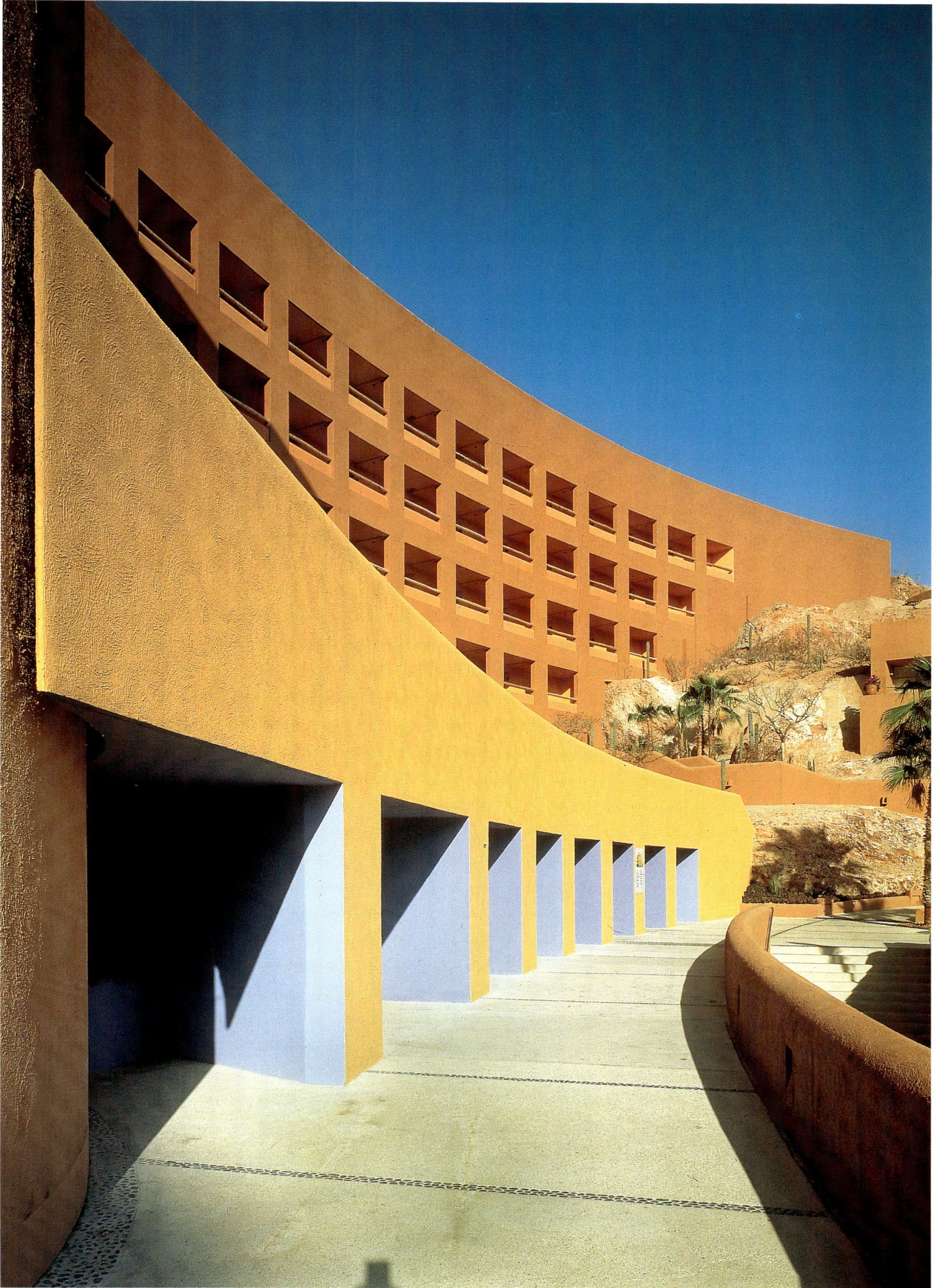

51

One exterior views
of the condominiuns
and detail of front
elevation.

Top of page, main
building elevation
and, bottom of page,
two impressing images
of how the complex
blends in with nature.

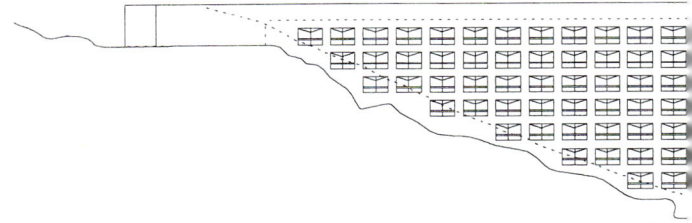

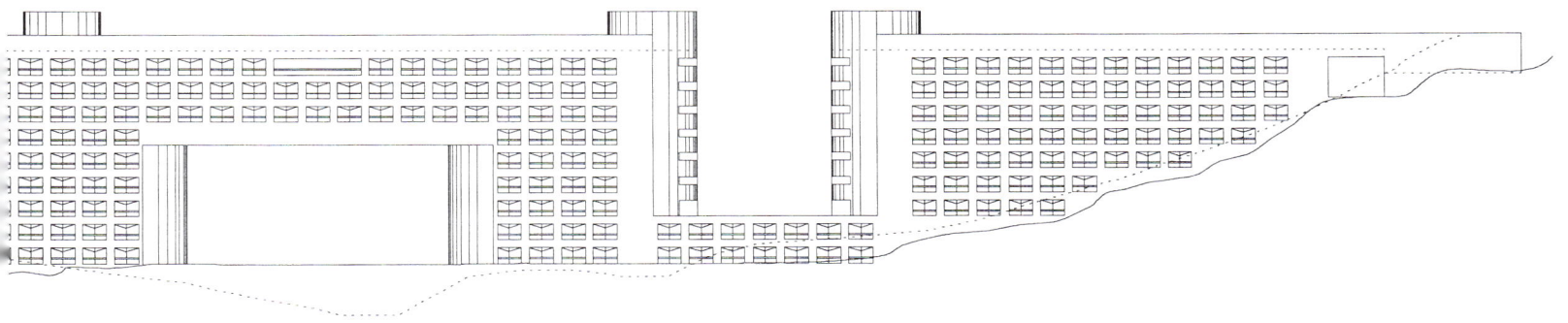

Malinalco Golf Club Villas

Owner
Club de Golf Malinalco, A.C.

Ground area
35,800.00 sq/m

Constructed area
7,500 sq/m

Architectural Design
de Yturbe Arquitectos

Collaborator
Luís Alberto Torres

Structural Project
Club de Golf Malinalco

Electrical Project
Club de Golf Malinalco

Hydrological Project
Club de Golf Malinalco

Construction
Promueve

Lighting and Audio Design
Gustavo Cota Pérez

Text
Enrique Martin-Moreno

This project was planned for the motor lobby of the residential villas of the Malinalco Golf Club, also designed by de Yturbe Arquitectos. Two tall straight walls, that emerge from the ground, will direct the visitor to the motor lobby by passing a cylindric wall reflected in a shallow pool. An opening in the cylindric wall will admit the visitor to the courtyard, an empty cylindrical space contained by the circular wall, partly sheltered by a sloping roof. A horizontal slot in the cylindrical wall will allow the interior space to flow, and to joyously join the spectacular landscape provided by the golf course and the Malinalco scenery.

A vertical slot in the wall will allow one of the straight entrance walls to invade the interior space while the rectangular shallow pool will serve as a mirror, reflecting this serene space to the sky.

To the west of the courtyard once again will appear one of de Yturbe Arquitectos signatures: creating a skylight to flood with natural light the covered area of the courtyard, reclining a part of the cylindrical wall to form the steps, reminiscent of those found in pre-Columbian architecture, and placing clay flower pots on them.

Also to the west, a rectangular volume will house the offices needed for the golf club administration.

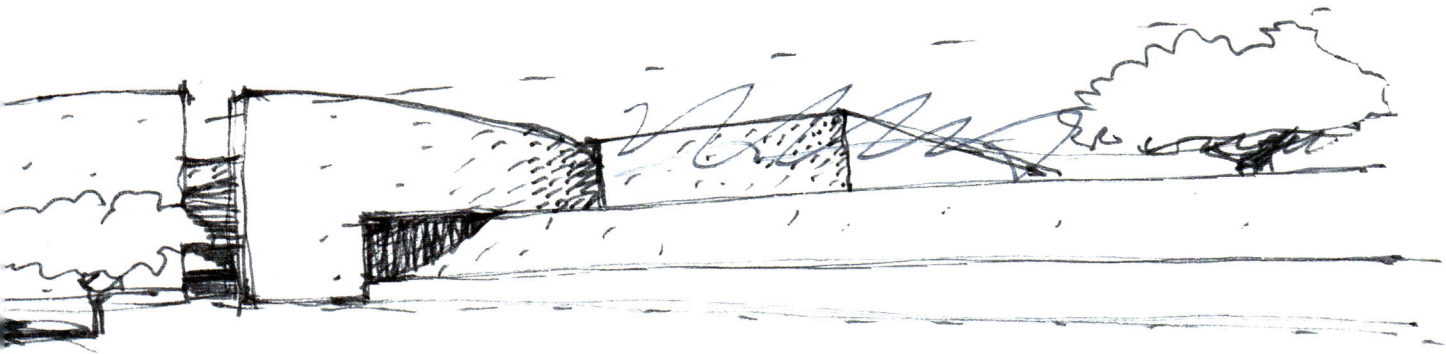

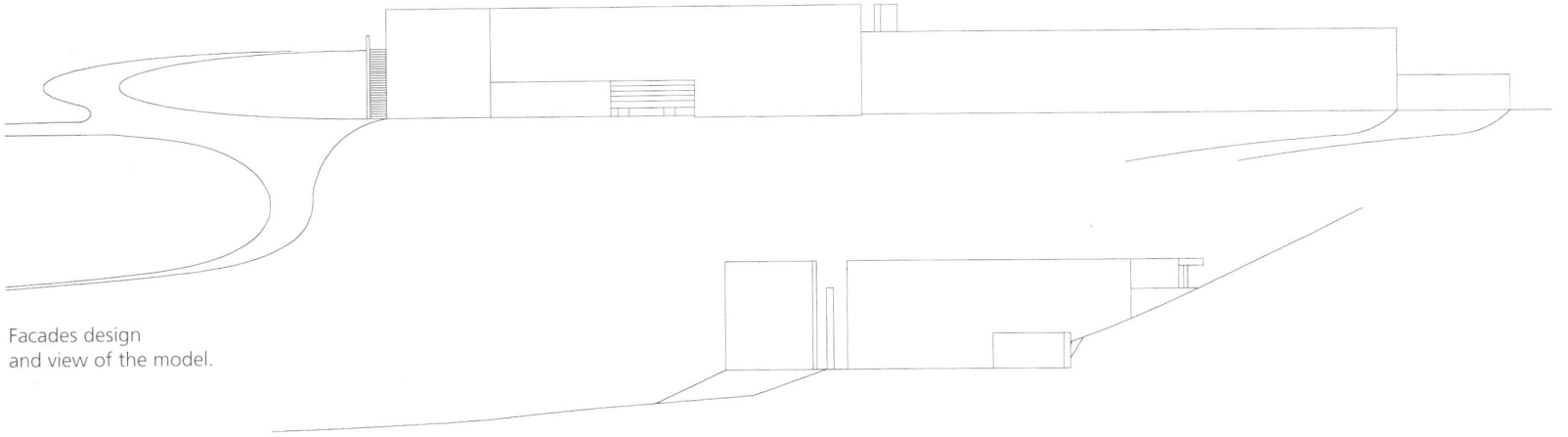

Facades design
and view of the model.

Section, plan at main level, and the natural environment around the complex.

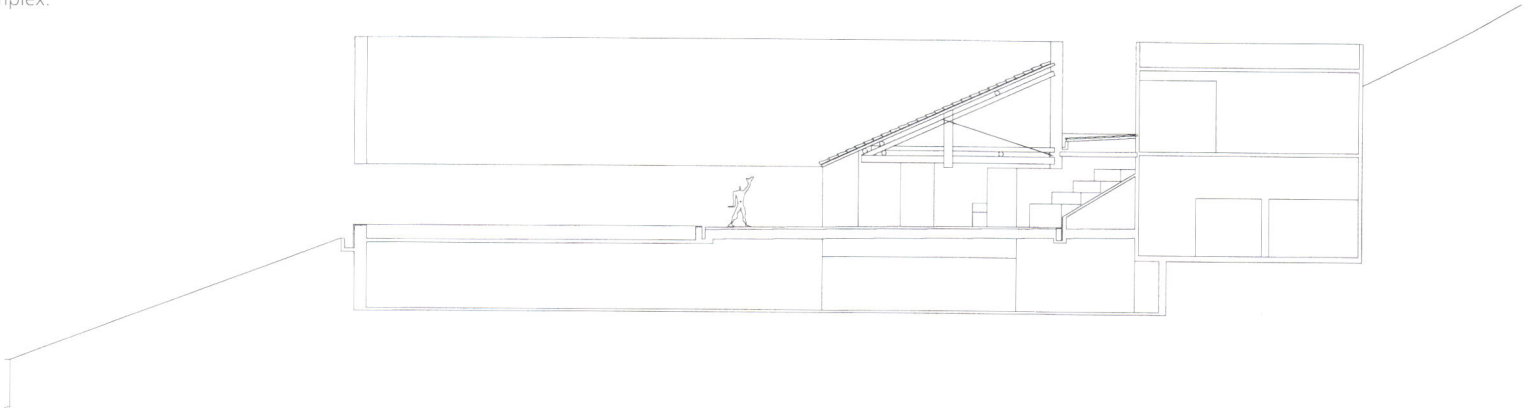

Monterrey, Nuevo Leon,
Mexico

Bancomer Office Building

Owner
Bancomer, S.A.

Ground area
5,970.00 sq/m

Constructed area
21,840.00 sq/m

Architectural Design
de Yturbe Arquitectos

Collaborator
Lucio Muniain

Project Development
1992

Renderings
Armando Ruíz Oteo

Text
Enrique Martin-Moreno

On the adjacent lot of the Torre Alta Office Building, Bancomer, one of Mexico's largest banks, planned to build an office building.

The project was solved as a cube of reflecting glass. The was a desire to have open terraces on the roof of the building, therefore the higher levels of the building were cut diagonally following the geometry of the Torre Alta building.

In order to complete the cubic form   of the building, a Mexican pink grid structure was overlapped on top of the glass volume.

The result would have been an unsurpassed interior space furnished by astonishing views of the city of Monterrey, and an example of integration between two independent urban-oriented buildings.

The grid structure overlapped on top of the building to complete its cubic form. Below, general plan.

Opposite page, two views of model.

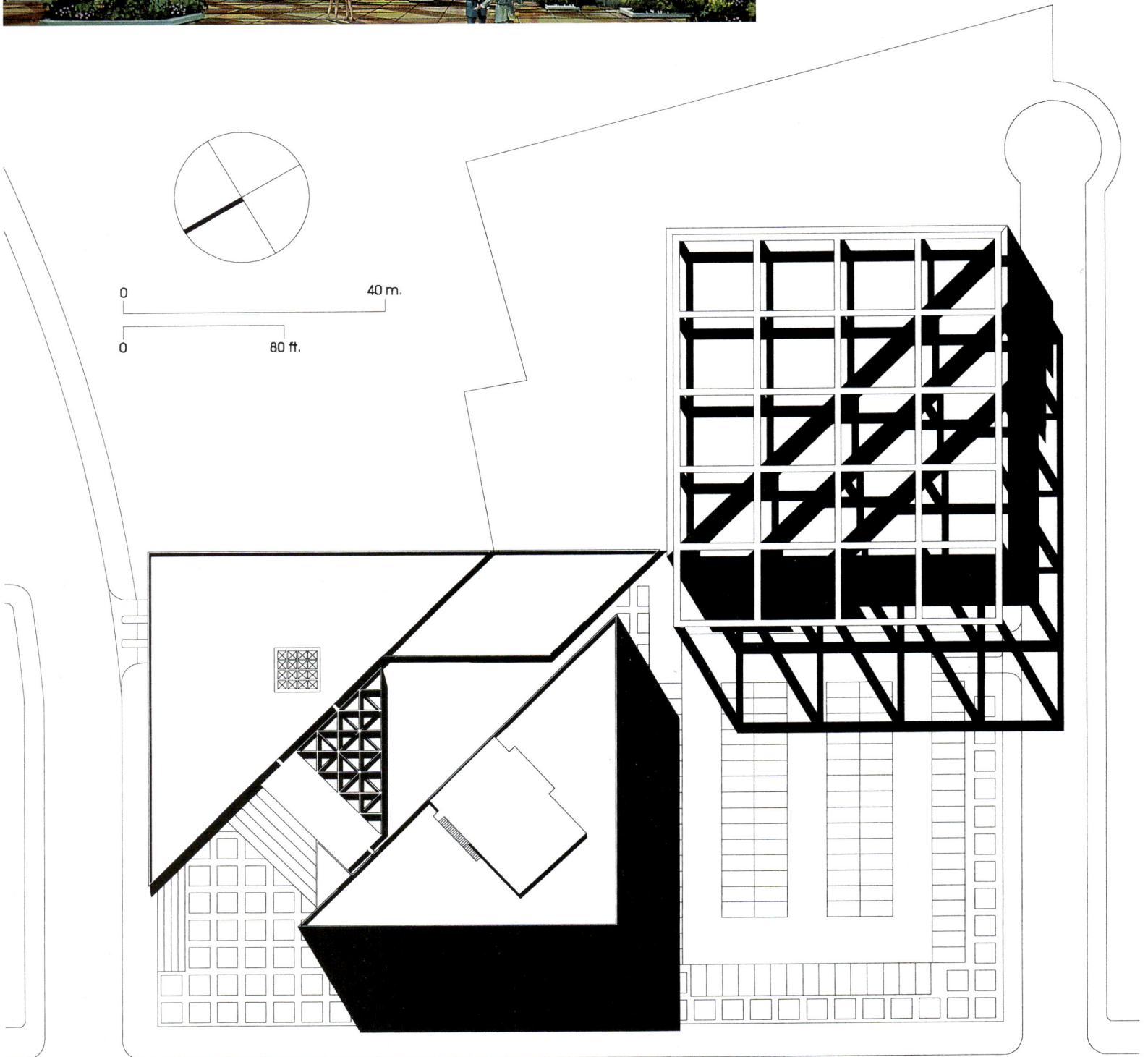

0   40 m.

0   80 ft.

House in Valle de Bravo

Ground area
1,308.00 sq/m

Constructed area
608.000 sq/m

Beginning construction date
1994

Opening date
1995

Architectural Design
de Yturbe Arquitectos

Collaborator
Andrés Cajiga

Structural Project
Francisco Tapia Ingenieros

Electrical Project
E.L.E. Instalaciones Electromecánicas

Hydrological Project
E.L.E. Instalaciones Electromecánicas

Construction
De Yturbe Arquitectos

Architectural supervision
De Yturbe Arquitectos Pablo
Sepúlveda

Project Development
1994

Interior Design
De Yturbe Arquitectos

Text
Enrique Martin-Moreno

Valle de Bravo is a well-known lakeside weekend retreat for Mexico City residents, located in a valley just a couple of hours away from the nation's capital. It is a place with strong vernacular architecture. The lakeside town of Valle de Bravo has stone paved streets, the houses are painted white with red dadoes and tiled roofs. The climate of Valle de Bravo is warm and sunny during the day all year round, but during the evenings it tends to get a bit chilly.

This house, situated on the outskirts of the town, on a very steep ravine, was originally built by de Yturbe in 1973, the remodeling project was done in 1993. The whole house was designed to enjoy the beautiful vistas provided by the lake and the mountains that surround the Valle de Bravo valley, making the outside an intricate part of the inside of the house.

A discreet door in the protective street wall admits the visitor to a flight of steps which leads down to a clay paved courtyard, an empty cube within a cube of plain walls. You then discover the beautiful view of the lake framed by two roughly carved pine columns that hold the timber beams that support the slanting tiled roof of the open terrace. This great terrace, the "heart" of the house during the evenings, with its clay and cobbled flooring, is typical of de Yturbe Arquitectos. It is here that the dining room and living room are situated. The living room has

a large circular fireplace that fights the lakeside chill, surrounded by a built-in sofa and *equipales* (traditional Mexican round chairs made out of wood and leather).

The large stone coffee table has a carved curve-line that holds water and reflects the fire when the fireplace is lit. The terrace lacks ornament, aside from the occasional cluster of clay flowerpots, but here one can enjoy the warmth and coziness of a traditional weekend retreat due to the warmth and the craftwork of the materials used in its construction.

From the terrace, through a covered staircase, you reach the bedrooms from where you can also enjoy the beautiful view of the lake.

Continuing down these covered stairs you reach what is the most popular space during the day: the swimming pool, that works as a mirror and seems to unite the lake and the mountains to the house. Surrounded by dense vegetation, the pool area becomes enveloped by nature.

Plans of entrance level,
level minus two,
and terrace level.

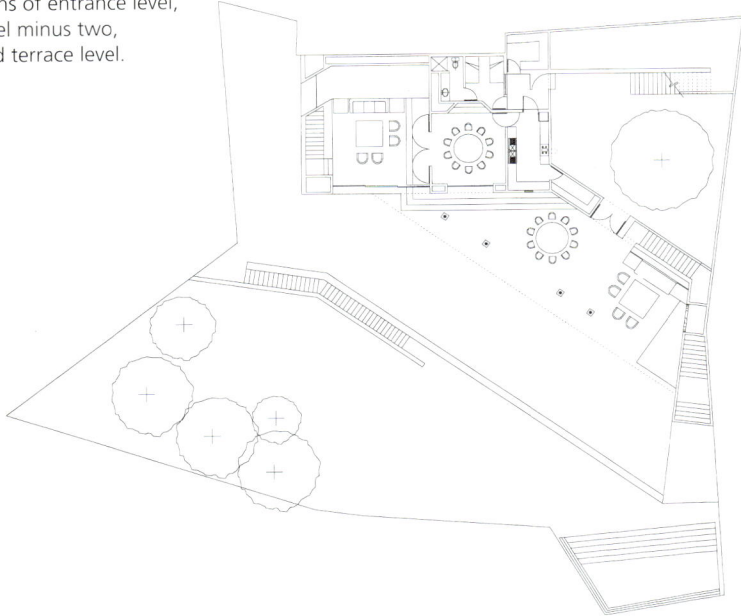

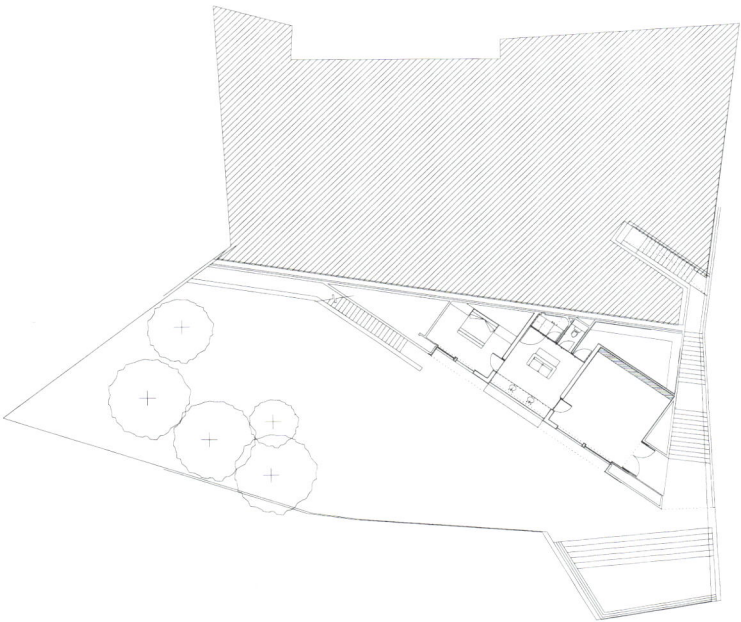

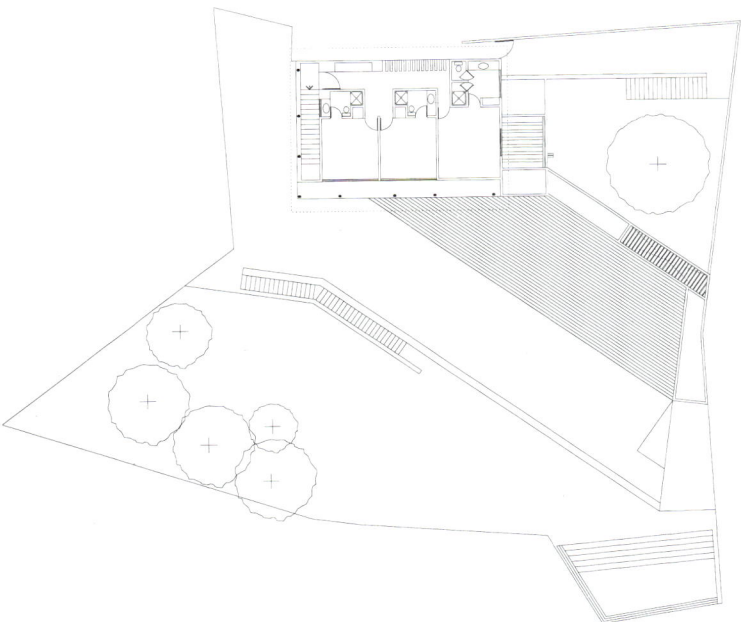

Two views of the terrace.

The large iron entrance
gate which, opposite
page, opens into the
inside of the building.

House in Las Lomas

Ground area
1,022.00 sq/m

Constructed area
1,660.00 sq/m

Beginning construction date
1995

Opening date
1996

Architectural Design
de Yturbe Arquitectos

Architectural Team
Karla Arana, Luís Alberto Torres,
Roberto Otero, Ignacio de la Fuente.

Structural Project
Francisco Topia Ingenieros

Electrical Project
E.L.E. Instalaciones Electromecánicas

Hydrological Project
E.L.E. Instalaciones Electromecánicas

General Contractor
Gustavo Cota Pérez

Architectural Supervisor
De Yturbe Arquitectos

Lighting and Sound Project
Gustavo Cota Pérez

Air Conditioning
Calefacción y Ventilación, S.A. (CYVSA)

Text
Enrique Martin-Moreno

Las Lomas, which means "the hills", is one of the most exclusive neighbourhoods in the west of Mexico City. The house is located between two steep ravines, so it is built mainly below street level, and it enjoys wonderful views of the luxuriantly vegetated ravines. The house faces south and is always filled with light. This work by de Yturbe Arquitectos is a journey through different sensations in space.

A large wooden door admits the visitor to an ample corridor flanked by two tall vividly coloured walls with a framed tree-covered view of the ravine. A vertical opening in one of the walls admits to what would have been another corridor, except for the fact that one of the walls has been inclined and broken into vertical and horizontal planes, which resemble the steps found in pre-Columbian temples.

De Yturbe has placed maguey plants on these pseudo-steps, creating what seems to be a tribute to sun, sky and Mexican vegetation. This courtyard leads to a cylindrical reception area with massive plain walls and a highly textured stone flooring. This reception area leads to another cylindrical skylit space with a descending flight of steps that has horizontal openings that flood with light the lower levels of the staircase. The descent brings to a rectangular, naturally illuminated, vestibule on the lower level that houses the bedrooms of the house.

By continuing down the cylindrical staircase, one reaches a circular vestibule. From it, by passing through an ample corridor with a generous view of the courtyard, one reaches the living room. A square opening in one of the walls has a sliding window with a courtyard view. A square balustrade, placed under the window as if it were the missing part of the wall, flanks the entrance to the living room. The living room has a sliding window that opens to a small terrace overlooking the ravine.

From the circular vestibule on this level, one can also enter a gigantic cylindrical skylit library dug into the ground. The library is furnished in typical de Yturbe Arquitectos manner: with shelves made out of generous wood sections forming a grid pattern. The library has a large cross-shaped sliding window with a view of the coutyard.

The courtyard has a triangular shallow pool that works as a mirror reflecting the simple volumes of the house. The floor of the courtyard is made out of huge square boulders of a local black stone with white marble borders, creating a rectangular pattern.

From the library, by going down a majestic skylit flight of steps that works as a vestibule, one reaches the master bedroom with a large sliding window that opens to the beautifully landscaped backyard.

Plans of the fourth,
third, second,
and ground floors.

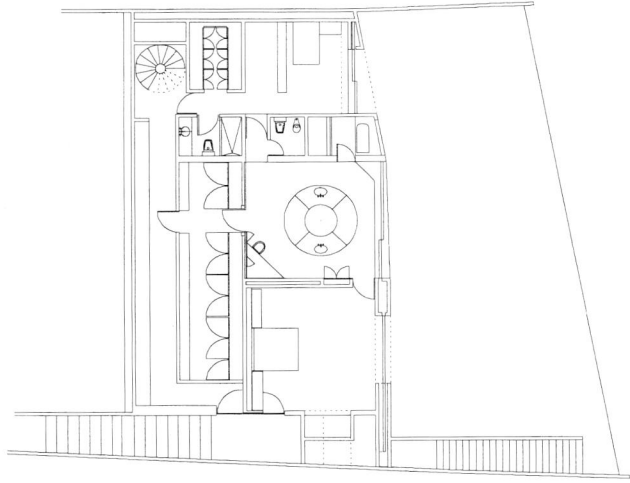

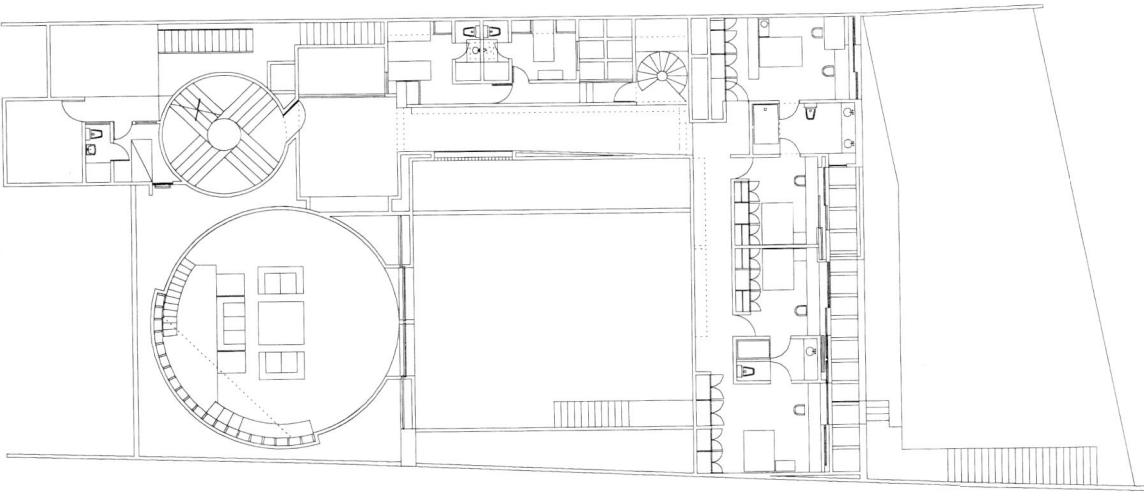

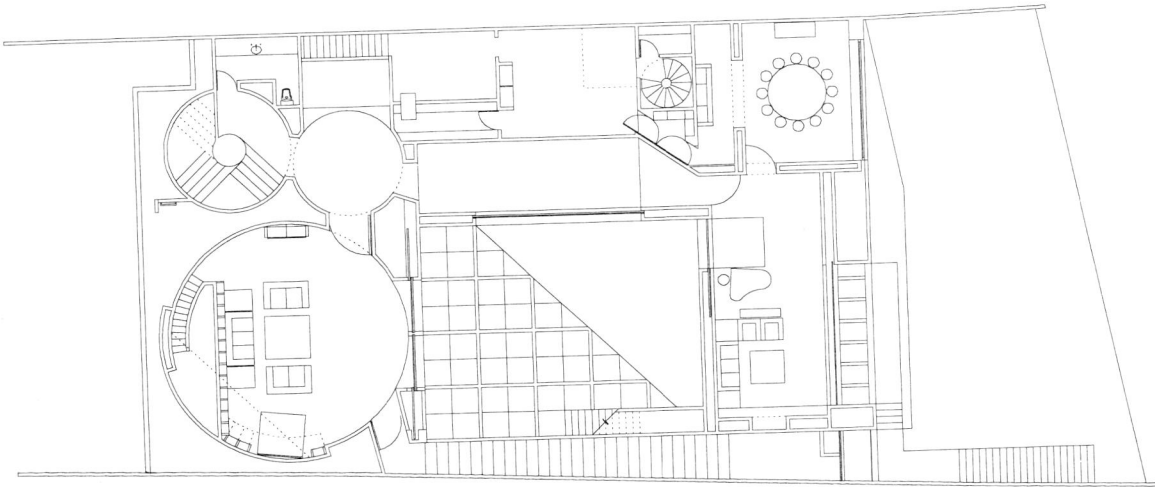

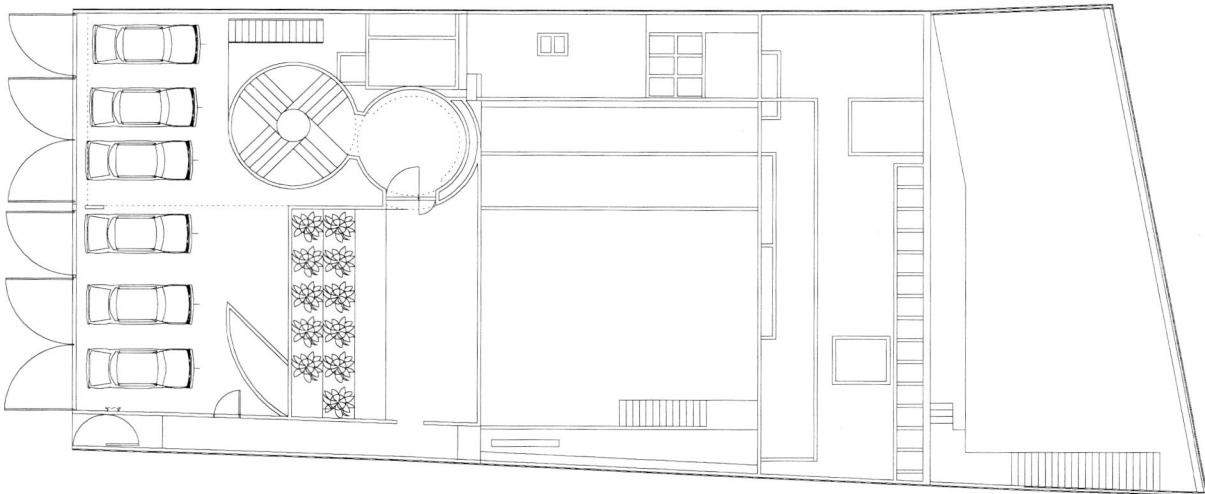

0 ———— 10 m.

0 ———— 20 ft.

The internal courtyard
showing its elegant
blend of colours.

Even the landscaping
contributes to the
architecture's elegant
interplay of colours.

The Banco Mexicano Corporate Head Office

Owner
Banco Mexicano

Ground area
690.00 sq/m

Constructed area
822.00 sq/m

Beginning construction date
1996

Opening date
1996

Architectural Design
de Yturbe Arquitectos

Collaborator
Mauricio de la Peña

Architectural Team
Mario Almino, Enrique Martín Moreno C.
Pablo Torresarpi.

Structural Project
Francisco Tapia Ingenieros

Electrical Project
Ingeniería Abel García

Hydrological Project
E.L.E. Instalaciones Electromecánicas

Construction
Marca Arquitectos

Architectural Supervision
De Yturbe Arquitectos

Project Development
1995

Lighting Project
Gustavo Cota

Text
Enrique Martin-Moreno

This bank will be located in a very commercial street, near the Dupuis store, in Mexico City.

The bank presents a tall massive white wall towards the street, parallel to the streetline. A vertical opening creates naturally illuminated and ventilated circulation in the interior, while a single square opening marks the entrance to the bank. An immense skylight with lowers floods with indirect natural light the third floor office area.

The bank has an empty court in front of the facade, where a circular staircase ascends from the underground parking lot.

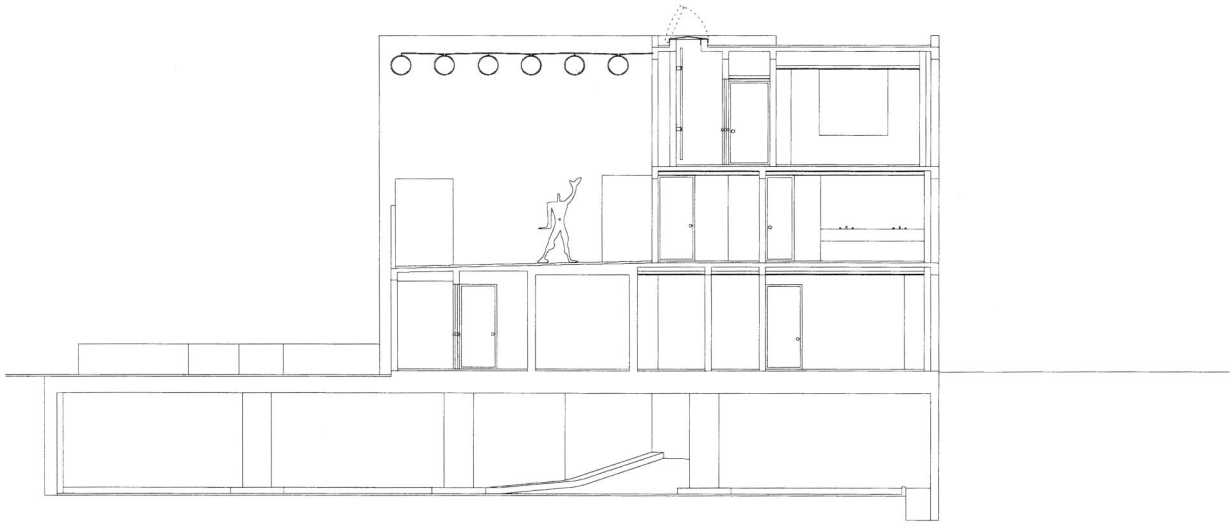

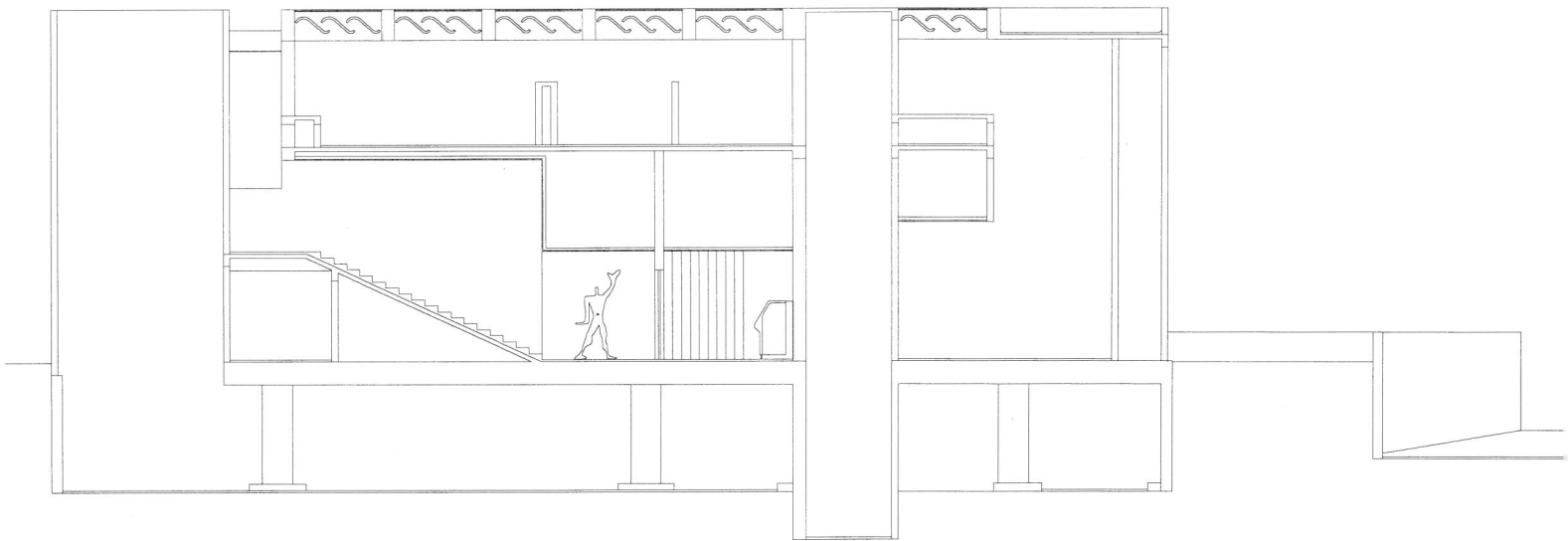

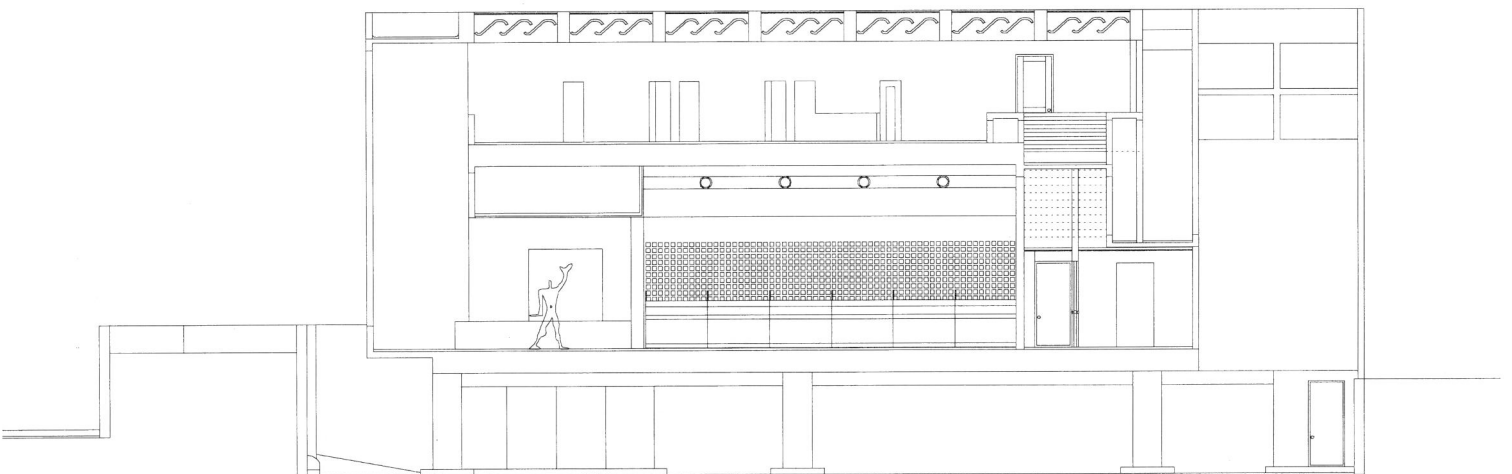

Opposite page, cross
section of the building.
This page, general plan
and plans of the second
floor and mezzanine
floor.

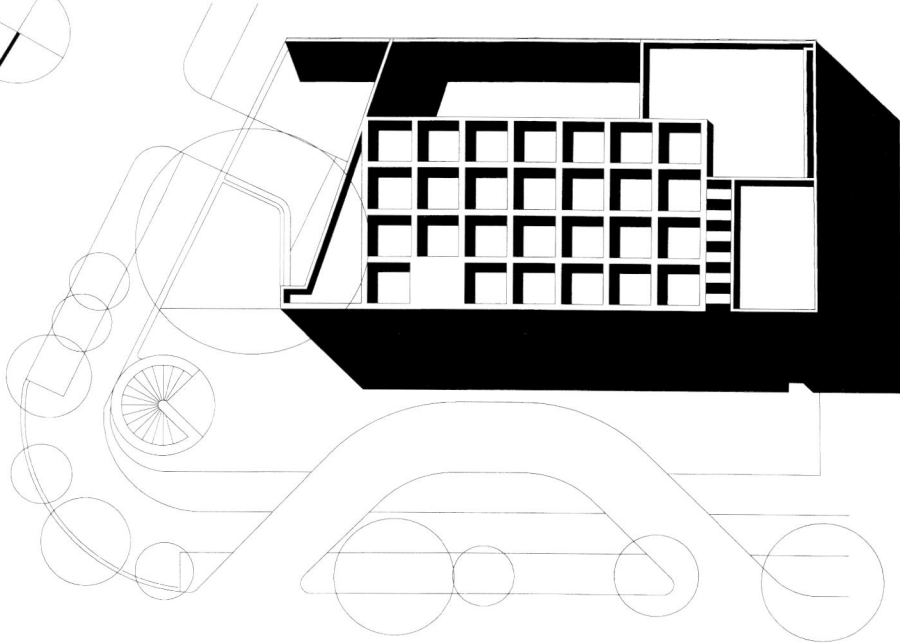

0   10 m.

0   20 ft.

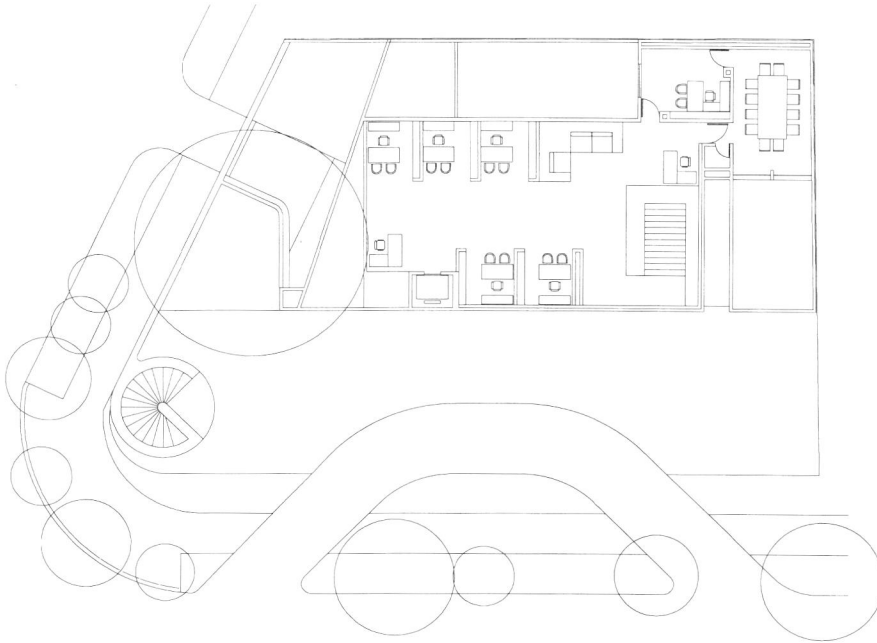

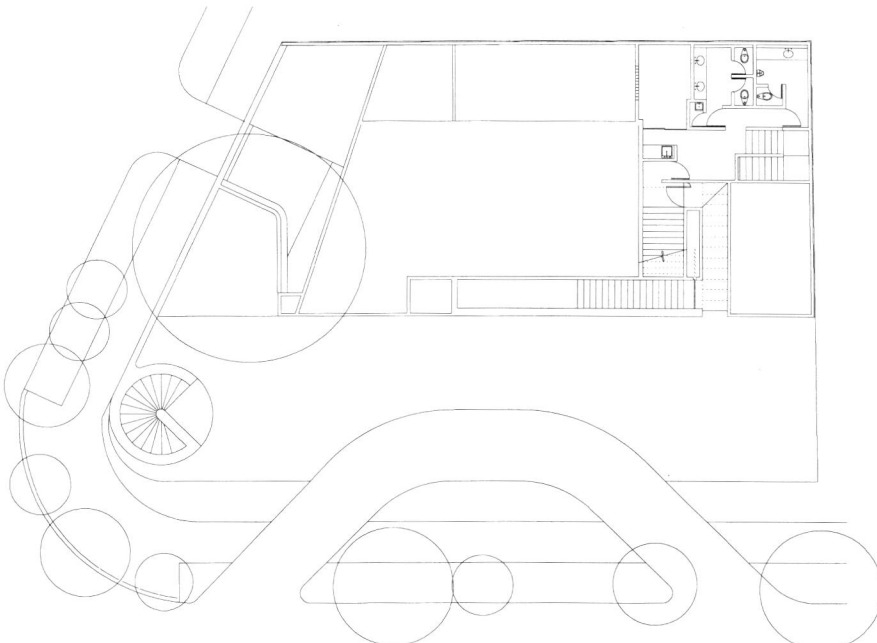

National Museum of Korea

Owner
Ministry of Culture & Sports Seoul Korea

Ground area
343.000.00 sq/m

Projected constructed area
75.000.00 sq/m

Architectural Design
de Yturbe Arquitectos

Collaborators
Mauricio de la Peña, Andrés Cajiga,
Luìs Alberto Torres, Karla Arana

Competition Date
1995

Project Development
Luìs Alberto Torres

Text
Lucio Muniain

In agreement with The National Museum of Korea's interest in recognizing the unique character of the Yongsan Family Park, we have taken the presence of the Han river and the understanding of both specific and general urban contexts as two primary influences for the design of our building.

Our design addresses the river and the city, not only in terms of views that are offered, but also in terms of the thematic associations they suggest. The formal gestures and activities of our building are, we believe, the creation of an *entrance to Korea's art and culture*: a physical, visual, psychological, emotional and ideal entrance that will represent Korea's national identity, an entrance that will work as a monument, an urban focus, and landmark.

This great Entrance to Korea's art and culture was conceived with the idea that a museum is born on the concept of artistic patrimony. Although this main entrance will work as a symbol for the artistic patrimony of Korea, we intend to have the curatorial and administrative building adjacent to it, so it sculptoric idea will be transformed into architecture.

This museum will offer the freedom and flexibility the museographer needs without taking away its image of permanency, which it must have.

It is formed by halls that can be integrated one with the other. In this way museography has all the options: to characterize space (according to the concept of hall) for a unitary ensemble of pieces or open large perspectives to relate distant pieces in the museographical discourse.

The light is a very important factor on the inside of the museum, therefore it has been handled well, making use of patios, gardens, skylights, domes or openings, giving the visitor a stimulating environment and lack of monotony. It is very important to emphasize the natural lighting of the museum since the direct use of sunlight will damage the pieces in a museum, this is why all the lighting proposed in this project will be indirect, avoiding direct sunlight.

The concept of having built-in ponds as landscape in the main lead to the museum is to achieve and create a character of permanency. Since the flooding of the Han river is a matter to take in good consideration, we thought that these permanent ponds will always look the same, with or without flooding, so that the visitor could freely visit the museum, and also they will protect the museum from any climatological disorder.

The creation of a great wall on the main walkway at the pedestrian entrance of the building will reinforce the concept of an anti-flood museum.

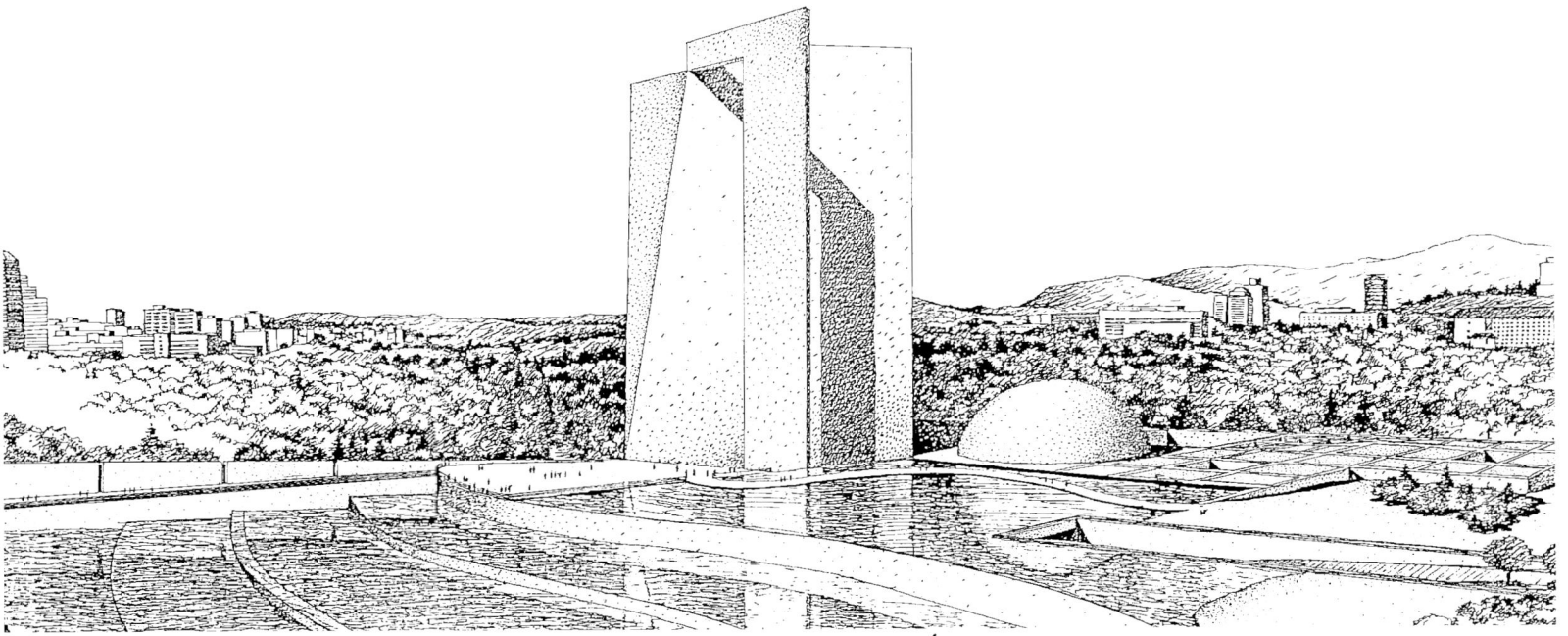

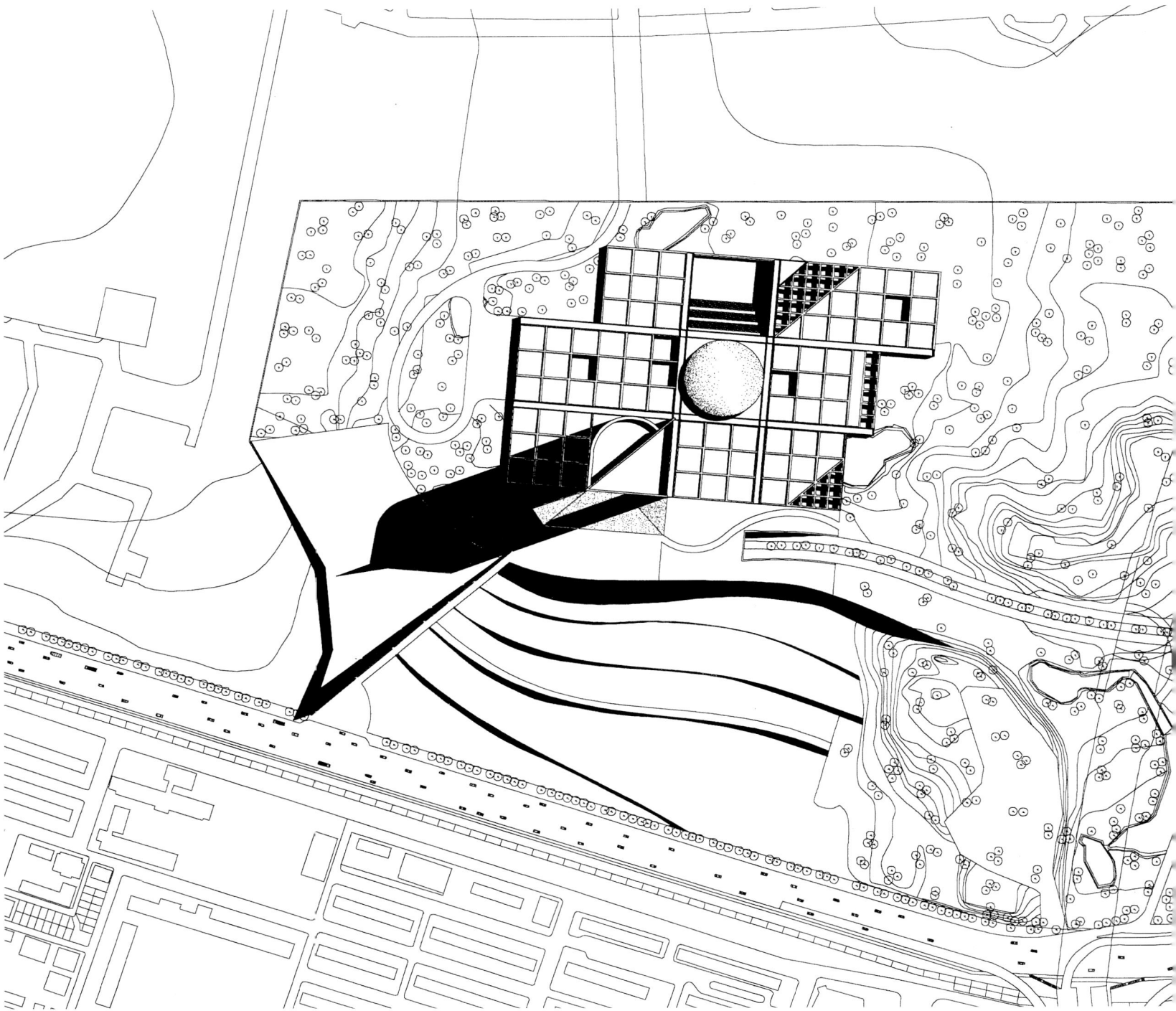

Opposite page general view and site plan. This page, two building plans.

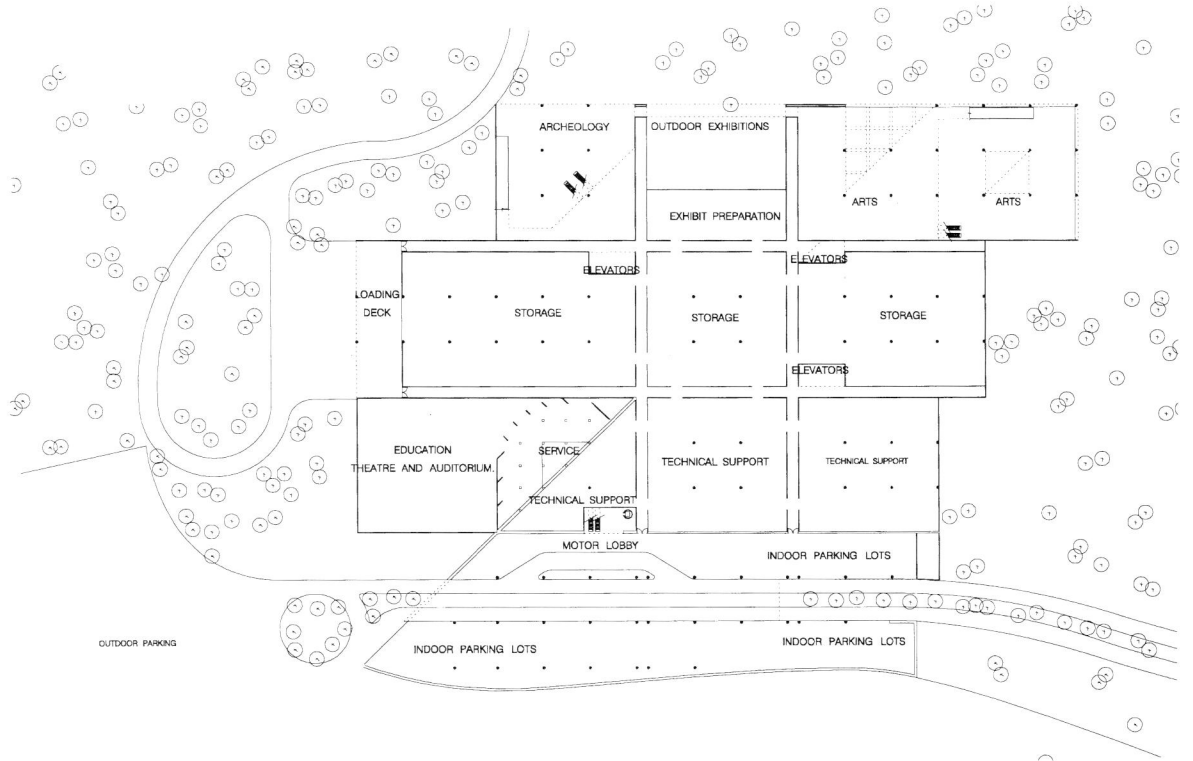

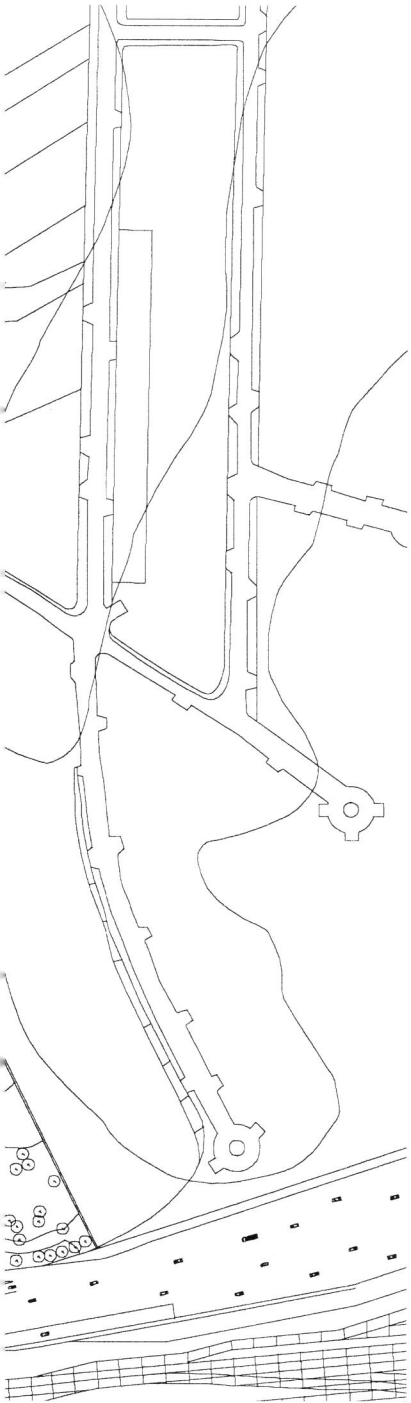

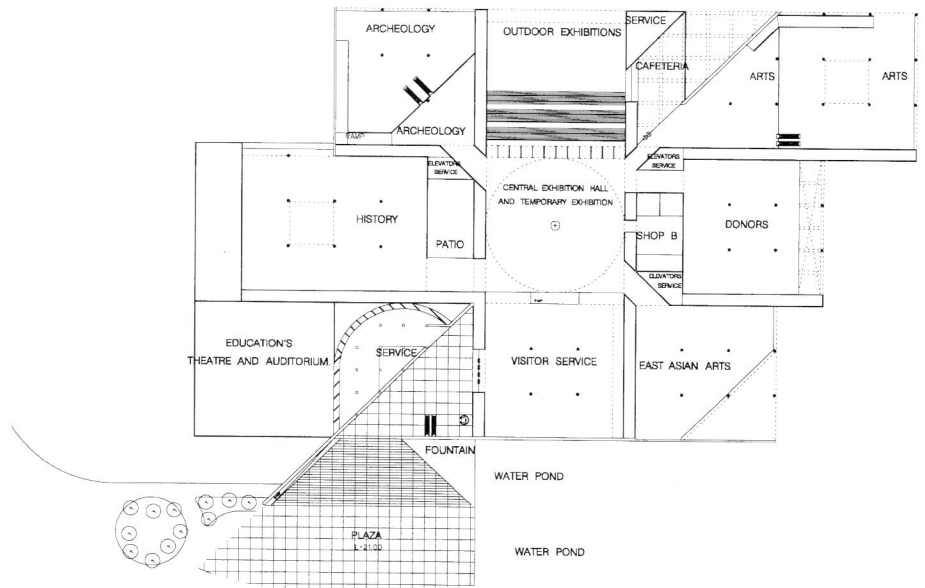

ARCHEOLOGY OUTDOOR EXHIBITIONS ARTS ARTS
EXHIBIT PREPARATION
ELEVATORS ELEVATORS
LOADING DECK STORAGE STORAGE STORAGE
ELEVATORS
EDUCATION THEATRE AND AUDITORIUM. SERVICE TECHNICAL SUPPORT TECHNICAL SUPPORT
TECHNICAL SUPPORT
MOTOR LOBBY INDOOR PARKING LOTS
OUTDOOR PARKING
INDOOR PARKING LOTS INDOOR PARKING LOTS

ARCHEOLOGY OUTDOOR EXHIBITIONS SERVICE ARTS ARTS
CAFETERIA
ARCHEOLOGY
RAMP
ELEVATOR SERVICE ELEVATORS SERVICE
CENTRAL EXHIBITION HALL AND TEMPORARY EXHIBITION
HISTORY PATIO SHOP B DONORS
ELEVATORS SERVICE
EDUCATION'S THEATRE AND AUDITORIUM SERVICE VISITOR SERVICE EAST ASIAN ARTS
FOUNTAIN WATER POND
PLAZA L-21.00 WATER POND

87

The Malinalco Golf Club House

Ground area
55,000 sq/m

Constructed area
6,500.00 sq/m

Beginning construction date
1991

Opening date
1993

Architectural Design
Javier Sordo Madaleno, José de Yturbe

Collaborator
Luís de la Vega

Structural Project
Jaime Loyola

Electrical Project
Hubard & Bourlon

Hydrological Project
G.H.A. Gutiérrez Tello y Asociados

Construction
CORPEC

Architectural Supervison
Sordo Madaleno Arquitectos

Interior Design
Sordo Madaleno Arquitectos

Landscape Architecture
Mario Schetnan

Urban Planning
Edward Stone Jr. & Associates (EDSA)

Lighting and Sound Design
Gustavo Cota Pérez

Text
Enrique Martin-Moreno

The Malinalco Golf Club was designed to provide an alternative weekend retreat for Mexico City's residents. Malinalco is situated in a valley surrounded by breathtaking mountains and luscious vegetation, just a couple of hours away from Mexico City. Its historical sites include an Aztec ceremonial centre that dates back to pre-Columbian times, a Romanesque Spanish monastery from colonial days, and a picturesque town with stone-paved streets, slanting tiled roofs and vernacular houses painted in vivid colours. The Golf Club is situated on the outskirts of the small town. It is there, in the middle of the golf course, standing out against a backdrop of majestic mountains, that we find the club house. As in all of de Yturbe's works, there is a powerful symbiosis with nature.

Following in the tradition of Mies Van der Rohe, the clubhouse walls project themselves towards indefinite points on the horizon, creating a sense of belonging to the surrounding scenery.

The materials used for the clubhouse are also deeply entrenched in the surroundings, reinterpreting the colonial town-style in a more contemporary Mexican architectural idiom. Entering the clubhouse, you are greeted by a typical Mexican courtyard revisited in de Yturbe's minimalist style.

Although the courtyard lacks ornamentation, the warmth of the space is created by the materials. The warm timber beams holding up the slanting roof, the craftsmanship of the tiled roof, the texture of the cobbled floors, and the colours of the massed walls are a feast for the senses. The courtyard also contains one of de Yturbe Arquitectos' signature features: one of the walls of the courtyard has been broken and inclined to create a skylight. This inclined plane is then split into horizontal and vertical planes reminiscent of the steps of a prehispanic pyramid.

The fountain in the centre of the courtyard evokes the serenity of a Japanese garden, with the perpetual movement of water creating concentric circles around the stone sphere in the centre of the fountain.

This courtyard exemplifies the notion that silence does not necessarily mean no-sound, for the sound made by the motion of the water, or even the sound of children playing in the courtyard, blend in to an almost poetic sense of tranquillity.

The balance between openness and closure epitomized in the clubhouse is perhaps unique. Although the project lives from within, it evolves around perpendicular axes drawing us towards the beautiful vistas on the outside. The tall corridors covered with skylights have timber logs placed horizontally from wall to wall to create a sense of shelter from the open sky. The logs cast shadows that change the shades of colour on the wall, seemingly shortening the length of the corridor.

General plan of complex.

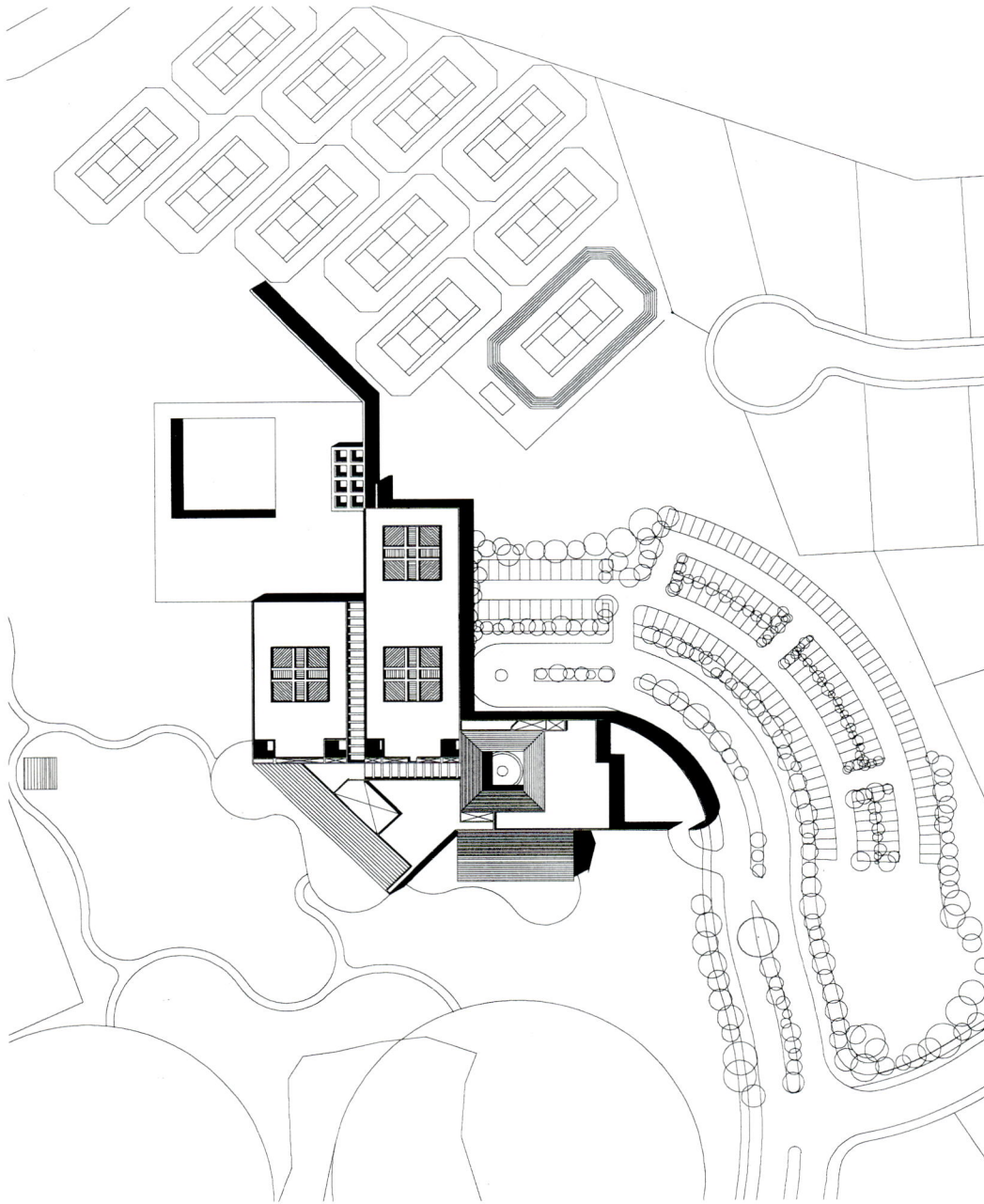

0   100 m.

0   200 ft.

Longitudinal section
of building and, below,
an external view.

WITHDRAWN

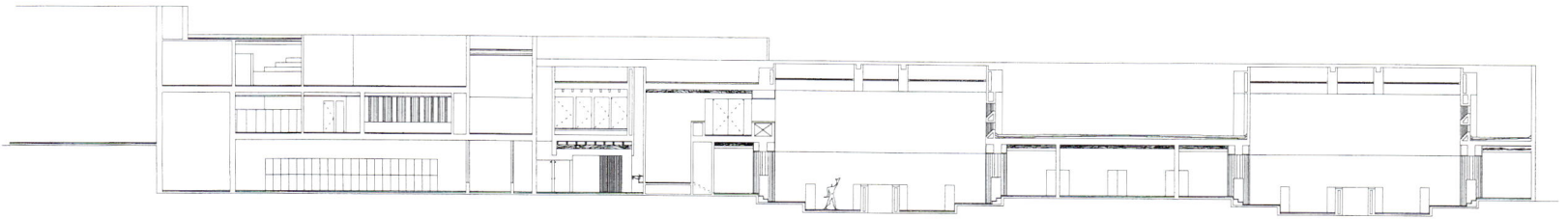

0   20 m.

0   40 ft.

Inside of patio.
Opposite page,
an internal passage
of complex.

Another view
of complex's internal
spaces.

Marco Polo describes a bridge,
stone by stone.
"But which is the stone that supports the whole
bridge?" asks Kublai Kan.
"The bridge is not held by this stone or that
one" answers Marco "but by the line in the
arch they form."
Kublai Kan remains silent, thinking.
Then he adds:
"Why do you talk to me about stones?"
"All that matters is the arch."
Marco Polo replies, "Without stones there is no
arch."

Italo Calvino
Traslated from "Le città invisibili"

We would like to borrow these words from Italo Calvino to thank Andres Cajiga, Mauricio De La Pena, Luis Alberto Torres, Karla Arana, Enrique Martin Moreno, Mario Almino, Santiago Lopez Silanes, Roberto Ramirez, Gerardo Sanchez, Pablo Torresarpi, Roberto Otero, Manuel Cervantes, and all the architects that in some form or another have been involved in this architectural team for their undying effort and endless contributions to the works we present to you.

To our clients and friends for their support and confidence.

To our consultants, for their knowledge and sharing experience.

To Pierantonio Giacoppo, l'Arca edizioni, and all their design team for this wonderful opportunity.

To Fernando Cordero, Paul Czitrom, Mario Mutschlechner and Arturo Zavala Haag for translating our architecture into images.

To the miniature architecture of Rafael Arellano and Arturo Rodriguez, outstanding model makers.

And to all the anonymous workers that have participated in the construction of our projects.

Many thanks

José De Yturbe and Lucio Muniain

List of works

WITHDRAWN

1968
JOSÉ DE YTURBE LIMANTOUR HOUSE
Valle de Bravo, México

1971
JESÚS MORALES SAVIGNON HOUSE
Valle de Bravo, México

JAVIER DE LA BARRA HOUSE
Valle de Bravo, México

1972
ALEJANDRO MTZ. GALLARDO HOUSE
San Angel, México, D. F.

1973
BERNARDO SEPÚLVEDA HOUSE
(House Carlos Fuentes)
San Jerónimo, México, D. F.

1974
GUEST HOUSE
Cía. Minera de Cananea
Cananea, Sonora, México
Project

MA. ESTHER ECHEVERRÍA HOUSE
San Jerónimo, México, D. F.

EDUARDO PRIETO SÁNCHEZ
MEJORADA HOUSE
San Angel, México, D. F.
Project

MAX GUTTMAN HOUSE
Lomas de Chapultepec, México, D. F.
Project

RODOLFO ECHEVERRÍA HOUSE
San Jerónimo, México, D. F.

ROBERTO PALACIOS HOUSE
San Angel, México, D. F.

1975
RESIDENTIAL COMPLEX
Paseos Taxqueña, México, D. F.
Project

EDMUNDO GIRAULT HOUSE
Bosques de las Lomas, México, D. F.

1976
JAVIER PRIETO SÁNCHEZ
MEJORADA HOUSE
San Angel, México, D. F.

MAXIMILIANO ECHEVERRÍA HOUSE
Lomas de Bezares, México, D. F.

MAURICIO MADERO, JR. HOUSE
Cancún, Quintana Roo, México
Preliminary project

CLUB DE GOLF SAN GIL HOUSE
Querétaro, Qro., México
with Juan Sordo Madaleno

PATRIA COMPLEX
Polanco, México, D. F.
with Juan Sordo Madaleno
with Francisco Serrano
Project

CLUB RAQUETA BOSQUES
Bosques de las Lomas, México, D. F.
Interior design

PARK PRINCESS RESTAURANT
Lomas de Chapultepec, México, D. F.
Interior design

1977
HOUSE BERNARDO SEPÚLVEDA
Valle de Bravo, Edo. de México

ROSA LUZ ALEGRÍA HOUSE
San Jerónimo, México, D. F.

FRANCISCO SUAREZ HOUSE
Bosques de las Lomas, México, D. F.

1978
ALBERTO REYNAUD HOUSE
Chiluca, Edo. de México

1979
EDUARDO HOLSNEIDER HOUSE
Bosques de las Lomas, México, D. F.

GRUPO CONDUMEX OFFICE BUILDING
Chimalistac, Edo. de México

MEXICAN HISTORY RESEARCH CENTER
Grupo Condumex
Chimalistac, Edo. de México

OCAMI, S. A. OFFICES
México, D. F.
Refurbishment project

CASA DE BOLSA CARLOS TROUYET
Anzúres, México, D. F.
Refurbishment project

PATRICIO MANGINO HOUSE
Bosques de las Lomas, México, D. F.

TWO COMMERCIAL SPACES
Lomas Anáhuac México, D. F.

ATLAS INSURANCE OFFICES
Centro Histórico, México, D. F.
Refurbishment project

1980
LUÍS AGUILAR BELL HOUSE
Careyes, Jalisco, México
Project

FERNANDO SENDEROS HOUSE
La Estadía, Edo. de México

HORIZONTAL HIDALGO 161 COMPLEX
San Angel, México, D. F.

1981
ELENA SUINAGA A. HOUSE
Bosques de las Lomas, México, D. F.

EDUARDO CALDERÓN HOUSE
Anzures, México, D. F.
Project

CASOLAR HOUSE
Manzanillo, Colima, México
Project

HOUSE IN FIRE ANGEL
Nuevo México, U.S.A.

1982
FERNANDO SENDEROS HOUSE
Bosques de las Lomas, México, D. F.
Project

HOUSE IN LA ESTADÍA, LOT 9
Grupo DESC
La Estadía, Edo. de México

HOUSE IN LA ESTADÍA, LOT 11
Grupo DESC
La Estadía, Edo. de México

EDMUNDO GIRAULT HOUSE
Valle de Bravo, Edo. de México

EDUARDO MESTRE HOUSE
Vista Hermosa, Edo. de México

MAGDALENA S. DE YTURBE HOUSE
Lomas de Chapultepec, México, D. F.
Refurbishment project

TORRE ALTA
Monterrey, N. L., México
1985 Architecture Biennial Prize
Colegio de Arquitectos de la Ciudad de
Nuevo León
Assistants: Jorge Garza, Fernando de Haro,
Bernardo Hinojosa

FIESTA AMERICANA HOTEL
Guadalajara, Jalisco, México
with Jorge Garza
with Fernando de Haro

1983
FRANCISCO MARTÍN MORENO HOUSE
Cuernavaca, Morelos, México
Project

JOSÉ LUÍS LAGUNA HOUSE
Valle de Bravo, Edo. de México

XAVIER AUTRAY HOUSE
Lomas de Chapultepec, México, D. F.

SUTI SUINAGA HOUSE
Lomas de Chapultepec, México, D. F.

FEDERICO CLASSING HOUSE
Vista Hermosa, México, D. F.

RODOLFO GARCÍA MURIEL HOUSE
Lomas de Chapultepec, México, D. F.
Refurbishment project

1984
GRUPO CONDUMEX OFFFICES
AND AUDITORIUM
Chimalistac, Edo. de México

ROBERTO HERNÁNDEZ HOUSE
Valle de Bravo, Edo. de México

CLAUDE D'SAYVE HOUSE
Park City, Utah, U.S.A.
Project

PATRICIO REYNAUD HOUSE
Bosques de las Lomas, México, D. F.

PATRICK DE SPA HOUSE
Valle de Bravo, México, D. F.

STURE GRAFFMAN HOUSE
Valle de Bravo, México, D. F.

1985
JUAN MANUEL ALONSO HOUSE
Bosques de las Lomas, México, D. F.

LARS CHRISTIANSON HOUSE
San Angel, México, D. F.

NORMA REDO DE YTURBE HOUSE
Valle de Bravo, Edo.de México

LARS CHRISTIANSON HOUSE
Bosques de las Lomas, México, D. F.

JAVIER PIZARRO HOUSE
México, D. F.

1986
MAGDALENA S. DE YTURBE HOUSE
Valle de Bravo, Edo. de México

MANUEL GONZÁLEZ SORDO HOUSE
Valle de Bravo, Edo. de México

RODOLFO GARCÍA MURIEL HOUSE
Valle de Bravo, Edo. de México
Refurbishment project

CONRAD HILTON HOTEL
Cancún, Quintana Roo, México
with Javier Sordo Madaleno
Project

1987
PAUL DAVIDOFF HOUSE
Valle de Bravo, Edo. de México

JUAN RIVEROLL HOUSE
Valle de Bravo, Edo. de México

GABRIEL GARCÍA MÁRQUEZ HOUSE
Chimalistac, Edo. de México

MARRIOT HOTEL
Pto. Vallarta, Jalisco, México

with Javier Sordo Madaleno
Competition project

PRESIDENTE HOTEL
Cancún, Quintana Roo, México
with Javier Sordo Madaleno
Extension and refurbishment project

LUÍS BARRIOS SÁNCHEZ HOUSE
Lomas de Chapultepec, México, D. F.

LUIS BARRIOS SÁNCHEZ HOUSE
Valle de Bravo, Edo. de México
Project

1988
ALBERTO OSIO HOUSE
Valle de Bravo, Edo. de México
Project

MIGUEL DE LARMINAT
COUNTRY HOUSE
Tipiluca, Argentina

ALEJANDRO LEGORRETA HOUSE
Valle de Bravo, Edo. de México

HÉCTOR LAGOS HOUSE
Valle de Bravo, Edo. de México
Project

LUÍS SUINAGA HOUSE
Valle de Bravo, Edo. de México

MARCOS CARRILLO A. HOUSE
Valle de Bravo, Edo. de México

RAFAEL AMBROSI HOUSE
Valle de Bravo, Edo. de México

GUILLERMO LAGOS HOUSE
Los Encinos, Edo. de México
Project

JUAN MOCH HOUSE
Valle de Bravo, Edo. de México
Preliminary project

CONRAD HILTON HOTEL
Pto. Vallarta, Jalisco, México
with Javier Sordo Madaleno
Competition project

1989
DE LAS PALAPAS HOUSE
Patzcuaritos, Nayarit, México

CONRAD HILTON HOTEL
Los Cabos, B. C. S., México
with Javier Sordo Madaleno
Competition project

1990
CONRAD HILTON HOTEL
Pto. Vallarta, Jalisco, México
with Javier Sordo Madaleno
Project

CONRAD HILTON HOTEL
Los Cabos, B. C. S., México
with Javier Sordo Madaleno
Project

1991
WESTIN REGINA HOTEL
Pto. Vallarta, Jalisco, México
with Javier Sordo Madaleno

WESTIN REGINA HOTEL
Los Cabos, B. C. S., México
with Javier Sordo Madaleno

1992
ROBERTO AVELAR HOUSE
Valle Escondido, Edo. de México

BANCOMER CORPORATE BUILDING
Monterrey, N. L., México
Project

1993
MIGUEL GÓMEZ HOUSE
San José, Costa Rica

MANUEL GÁRATE HOUSE
Valle Escondido, Edo. de México
Project

MALINALCO GOLF CLUB HOUSE
Malinalco, Edo. de México
with Javier Sordo Madaleno

MALINALCO GOLF CLUB -
TYPICAL HOUSE
Malinalco, Edo. de México
with Javier Sordo Madaleno
Project

1994
LA LOMA COMPLEX
APISA
Valle Escondido, Edo. de México
Project

PARQUE ESCONDIDO
RESIDENTIAL QUARTER
Inmobiliaria la Presa
Cuajimalpa, México
Competition project

OJEDA FRANCO HOUSE
Lomas de Chapultepec, México, D. F.
Refurbishing project
Preliminary project

GUEST HOUSE COSTA BANDERAS
Grupo Desk
Punta Mita, Nayarit, México
Competition project

Raúl Martínez Ostos House
San Angel, México, D. F.
Project

WITHDRAWN

BERNARDO SEPÚLVEDA HOUSE
Valle de Bravo, Edo. de México
Estension and refurbishing project

FELIPE YTURBE HOUSE
San Angel, México, D. F.
Refurbishing project

RANCHO SANTA FÉ
RESIDENTIAL COMPLEX
APISA
Santa Fé, México, D. F.
Preliminary project

GABRIEL CÁRDENAS DEPARTMENT
Frondoso, Edo. de México

LORAL, S. A. BUILDING
Lomas de Chapultepec, México, D. F.
Interior refurbishment project

DE YTURBE ARQUITECTOS OFFICE
Lomas de Chapultepec, México, D. F.

DUPUIS STORES
Phoenix, Arizona, U.S.A.
Guadalajara, Jalisco, México
Ave. Palmas, México, D. F.
Pedregal San Angel, México, D. F.
Refurbihing projects

SAZÓN RESTAURANT
Pto. Vallarta, Jalisco, México

1995
VILLAS MALINALCO DEVELOPMENT
CORPEC
Malinalco, Edo. de México
(on going)

URBAN DEVELOPMENT
Rancho San Diego
Valle de Bravo, Edo. de México
(on going)

THE NATIONAL MUSEUM OF KOREA
International Architectural Competition
Ministry of Culture and Sports
Seoul, Korea
Competition project

BANCO MEXICANO REGIONAL
HEAD QUARTERS
San Luís Potosí, S.L.P., México
(on going)

BANCO MEXICANO REGIONAL
HEAD QUARTERS
Chihuahua, Chih., México
(on going)

BANCO MEXICANO REGIONAL
HEAD QUARTERS
Puebla, Pue., México
(on going)

BANCO MEXICANO -
LOMAS DE CHAPULTEPEC AGENCY
México, D. F.
(on going)

FIESTA INN HOTELS
Facades of new hotels
(on going)

1996
MAGDALENA S. DE YTURBE HOUSE
Lomas de Chapultepec, México, D. F.

FIESTA AMERICANA
COZUMEL REEF VILLAS
Cozumel, Quintana Roo, México

HOTEL FIESTA
AMERICANA COZUMEL REEF
Cozumel, Quintana Roo, México
Refurbishing project
(on going)

LOCAL LAW COURTS
Suprema Corte de Justicia
Guadalajara, Jalisco, México
Competition project

RESIDENTIAL COMPLEX
GRUPO TERRUM
La Loma II
Santa Fé, México, D. F.
(on going)

CLUB DE YATES DE ACAPULCO
Acapulco, Guerrero, México
Refurbishing project
(on going)

VICTOR MANUEL MARTÍNEZ HOUSE
Veracruz, México
(on going)

TAMALLI RESTAURANT
Zona Rosa, México, D. F.
Refurbishing project

HUMBOLDT SCHOOL
City of Puebla, Puebla, Mexico
National Competition
(on going)

RESIDENTIAL COMPLEX
GRUPO TERRUM
MOLINO VIEJO II
Cuajimalpa, Mexico D.F.
(on going)

HOTEL IN CHINCHORRO
(40 SUITE)
GRUPO POSADAS
Quintana Roo, Mexico
(on going)

HOTEL IN KOHUNLICH
(60 KEYS)
GRUPO POSADAS
Quintana Roo, Mexico
(on going)

HOTEL IN PUNTA HERRADURA
(80 KEYS)
GRUPO POSADAS
Quintana Roo, Mexico
(on going)

HOTEL IN BOCA PAYLA
(80 KEYS)
GRUPO POSADAS
Quintana Roo, Mexico
(on going)

HOTEL IN CHEMUYIL
(200 KEYS)
GRUPO POSADAS
Quintana Roo, Mexico
(on going)

JUAN CARLOS BRANIFF HOUSE
Valle de Bravo, Edo. de Mexico
(on going)

IMPSAT OFFICE HEADQUARTERS
Interlomas, Edo. de Mexico
(on going)

REEF'S RESTAURANT
FIESTA AMERICANA COZUMEL
GRUPO POSADAS
Quintana Roo, Mexico
(on going)

CONDOMINIUM COMPLEX
Tres Vidas, Acapulco
National competition
(on going)

GRAND TOURISM HOTEL
GRUPO POSADAS
Los Cabos, B.C.S., Mexico
National Competition
(on going)

TAMALLI RESTAURANT
Polanco, Mexico D.F.
Refurbishing project

RESIDENTIAL COMPLEX
GRUPO LOMA
La Loma, Sta Fe, Mexico
(on going)

de Yturbe / arquitectos S.C.
José de Yturbe Bernal
Lucio Muniain

Monte Caucaso 915-501
Lomas de Chapultepec 11000 Mexico, D.F.
Tels (525) 5404368 5404398 5205912 5205916
Fax (525) 5208621
E-MAIL deyturbe@mail.teesa.com